The Russian Revolution

by
John M. Dunn

Lucent Books, P.O. Box 289011, San Diego, CA 92198-9011

Titles in the World History Series

The Age of Feudalism
Ancient Greece
Hitler's Reich
The Hundred Years' War
The Roman Empire
The Roman Republic
The Russian Revolution

Library of Congress Cataloging-in-Publication Data

Dunn, John M., 1949-
    The Russian revolution / by John M. Dunn.
    p. cm.—(World history series)
    Includes bibliographical references and index.
    Summary: Examines the people and events connected
to the Russian Revolution of 1917, particularly the role of
Vladimir Lenin.
    ISBN 1-56006-234-7 (alk. paper)
    1. Soviet Union—History—Revolution, 1917-1921—Juve-
nile literature. [1. Soviet Union—History—Revolution, 1917-
1921. 2. Lenin, Vladimir Il'ich, 1870-1924.] I.Title. II. Series.
DK265.D66   1994
947.084'1—dc20
                                                                93-22869
                                                                CIP
                                                                AC

Contents

Foreword

Each year on the first day of school, nearly every history teacher faces the task of explaining why his or her students should study history. One logical answer to this question is that exploring what happened in our past explains how the things we often take for granted—our customs, ideas, and institutions—came to be. As statesman and historian Winston Churchill put it, "Every nation or group of nations has its own tale to tell. Knowledge of the trials and struggles is necessary to all who would comprehend the problems, perils, challenges, and opportunities which confront us today." Thus, a study of history puts modern ideas and institutions in perspective. For example, though the founders of the United States were talented and creative thinkers, they clearly did not invent the concept of democracy. Instead, they adapted some democratic ideas that had originated in ancient Greece and with which the Romans, the British, and others had experimented. An exploration of these cultures, then, reveals their very real connection to us through institutions that continue to shape our daily lives.

Another reason often given for studying history is the idea that lessons exist in the past from which contemporary societies can benefit and learn. This idea, although controversial, has always been an intriguing one for historians. Those that agree that society can benefit from the past often quote philosopher George Santayana's famous statement, "Those who cannot remember the past are condemned to repeat it." Historians who ascribe to Santayana's philosophy believe that, for example, studying the events that led up to the major world wars or other significant historical events would allow society to chart a different and more favorable course in the future.

Just as difficult as convincing students to realize the importance of studying history is the search for useful and interesting supplementary materials that present historical events in a context that can be easily understood. The volumes in Lucent Books' World History Series attempt to present a broad, balanced, and penetrating view of the march of history. Ancient Egypt's important wars and rulers, for example, are presented against the rich and colorful backdrop of Egyptian religious, social, and cultural developments. The series engages the reader by enhancing historical events with these cultural contexts. For example, in *Ancient Greece,* the text covers the role of women in that society. Slavery is discussed in *The Roman Empire,* as well as how slaves earned their freedom. The numerous and varied aspects of everyday life in these and other societies are explored in each volume of the series. Additionally, the series covers the major political, cultural, and philosophical ideas as the torch of civilization is passed from ancient Mesopotamia and Egypt, through Greece, Rome, Medieval Europe, and other world cultures, to the modern day.

The material in the series is formatted in a thorough, precise, and organized manner. Each volume offers the reader a comprehensive and clearly written overview of an important historical event or period. The topic under discussion is placed in a broad, historical context. For example, *The Italian Renaissance* begins with a discussion of the High Middle Ages and the loss of central control that allowed certain Italian cities to develop artistically. The book ends by looking forward to the Reformation and interpreting the societal changes that grew out of the Renaissance. Thus, students are not only involved in an historical era, but also enveloped by the events leading up to that era and the events following it.

One important and unique feature in the World History Series is the primary and secondary source quotations that richly supplement each volume. These quotes are useful in a number of ways. First, they allow students access to sources they would not normally be exposed to because of the difficulty and obscurity of the original source. The quotations range from interesting anecdotes to far-sighted cultural perspectives and are drawn from historical witnesses both past and present. Second, the quotes demonstrate how and where historians themselves derive their information on the past as they strive to reach a consensus on historical events. Lastly, all of the quotes are footnoted, familiarizing students with the citation process and allowing them to verify quotes and/or look up the original source if the quote piques their interest.

Finally, the books in the World History Series provide a detailed launching point for further research. Each book contains a bibliography specifically geared toward student research. A second, annotated bibliography introduces students to all the sources the author consulted when compiling the book. A chronology of important dates gives students an overview, at a glance, of the topic covered. Where applicable, a glossary of terms is included.

In short, the series is designed not only to acquaint readers with the basics of history, but also to make them aware that their lives are a part of an ongoing human saga. Perhaps they will then come to the same realization as famed historian Arnold Toynbee. In his monumental work, *A Study of History,* he wrote about becoming aware of history flowing through him in a mighty current, and of his own life "welling like a wave in the flow of this vast tide."

Important Dates in the History of the Russian Revolution

1820	1830	1840	1850	1860	1870	1880	1890	19

1825
Radicals called Decembrists fail to topple czarist government under Nicholas I.

1848
Karl Marx writes *The Communist Manifesto*.

1861
Czar Alexander II abolishes serfdom.

1881
Alexander II is assassinated.

1894
Nicholas II becomes Russia's last czar.

1895
Lenin is arrested and exiled.

1898
Russian Social Democratic Labor party is formed.

1900
Lenin edits the radical publication *Iskra*, in Munich.

1902
Socialist Revolutionary party is formed.

1903
Split develops between the Mensheviks and the Bolsheviks.

1904
The Russo-Japanese War begins.

1905
Hundreds are killed on "Bloody Sunday"; Nicholas II sets up Duma; strikes and protests paralyze Russia; the first soviet is organized in St. Petersburg.

1907-1914
Russia suffers continuous social unrest, strikes, economic problems, and terrorist attacks.

1914
Russia enters World War I.

1915
Czar Nicholas takes command of the Russian troops; Rasputin influences government decisions; public distrust and anger toward the monarchy grows; Russia fares badly in the war.

1916
Rasputin murdered; czarist government faces crisis.

1917
During February Revolution, power falls to revolutionaries in Petrograd; Nicholas abdicates; Provisional Government shares power with Soviet Ex Com; Lenin returns to incite Bolshevik revolt; "July Days" shake Petrograd; Lenin flees Russia; Soviets aid Kerensky in suppressing Kornilov's revolt; Lenin returns to lead Bolshevik revolution; Bolsheviks enter Winter Palace, depose Provisional Government, and take control of the country.

1918-1921
Russian civil war is accompanied by Red Terror; Lenin imposes War Communism.

1918
Lenin signs Treaty of Brest-Litovsk, taking Russia out of World War I; Bolsheviks disband Constituent Assembly; Bolsheviks create a secret police, the Cheka; Bolsheviks renamed All-Russian Communist party, the Bolsheviks rule as dictators; Nicholas and family are executed.

1919-1943
Comintern attempts to position communism as world leader in socialism.

1921
Lenin introduces the New Economic Policy; Kronstadt revolt is suppressed by Communists.

1922
The Soviet Union is created.

1924
Lenin dies; Stalin wins struggle for leadership.

1925
Trotsky is stripped of power.

1927-1929
Stalin consolidates his power and assumes dictatorship.

1929-1932
Stalin launches collectivization of agriculture and massive industrialization plan; peasants resist and millions starve to death and otherwise succumb to Stalin's violent suppression.

1935-1938
Stalin presides over the Great Purge.

1940
Trotsky is assassinated in Mexico.

1953
Stalin dies.

1991
Soviet Union ceases to exist.

An Unfulfilled Promise

From 1905 to 1917, Russia's political, economic, and governmental system completely collapsed. Russia was marked by vast inequalities between its upper classes and the masses of poor peasants. This system began to crumble when peasants, impoverished workers, members of the middle class, soldiers, and sailors united to rebel against a government that tolerated famine and horrid working conditions, embroiled the country in unpopular, bloody wars, and imposed an oppressive political atmosphere in which human rights were ignored.

As Bruce Lockhart, the British consul-general in Moscow from 1915 to 1917 noted:

the [Russian] revolution took place because the patience of the Russian people broke down under a system unparalleled in inefficiency and corrup-

Russians call for political and economic reforms during a revolutionary parade in 1917. The ensuing revolution established the first communist state, the Soviet Union.

As leader of the Bolsheviks, Lenin, born Vladimir Ilyich Ulyanov, addresses crowds in Red Square.

conditions, better wages, and a form of government more responsive to their needs.

Unfortunately, they died and fought in vain. Out of the disorder and violence of the Revolution came a new breed of Russian rulers called the Bolsheviks. Led by a man named Vladimir Ilyich Ulyanov, who called himself V.I. Lenin, the Bolsheviks terrorized and oppressed the very classes in Russia that they promised to help. When Lenin died, a new dictator, Joseph Stalin, seized power. Stalin was a ruthless and murderous leader who killed millions of Soviet citizens in his monomaniacal quest to suppress opposition to his plans.

The new ruling philosophy was called communism, an economic and political system based on the ideas of Karl Marx, a German political philosopher. Within thirty years after the Russian Revolution, the nation was transformed from a backward agricultural land into an industrial superpower and a fearsome rival of the United States. Its influence in international matters stretched around the globe.

The Russian Revolution, noted John Reed, a young American journalist who was on the scene in 1917, was "[undeniably] . . . one of the great events of human history, and the rise of [the Bolsheviks], a phenomenon of worldwide importance."[2]

tion. No other nation would have stood the privations which Russia stood for anything like the same length of time.[1]

So, Russians rebelled and died by the thousands to secure for themselves peace, food, private property, improved working

1 Life Under the Czars

Before Russia collapsed in 1917, the empire had been ruled by a single powerful family, the Romanovs, for over 330 years. The empire consisted of 850 million square miles and extended across most of eastern Europe, matching an area about the size of North America. More than 140 million people lived within these borders including dozens of fiercely independent ethnic groups: Armenians, Balts, Finns, Jews, Germans, Poles, Ukrainians, and others.

Russia was large, backward, and undeveloped compared with other modern nations in western Europe, such as England and France. At a time when great changes were occurring in Europe, Russian development stagnated. In part, this was due to the influence of the Mongols, brutal nomadic attackers from Asia who had arrived

"Inhuman and Beastly"

An Englishman, Matthew Paris, described the Mongols in his work Chronica Majora *in 1259. The language in this excerpt has been modernized. It is taken from Ian Grey's* History of Russia.

"[The Mongols have] . . . poured forth like devils . . . razed cities, cut down forests, overthrown fortresses, pulled up vines, destroyed gardens, killed townspeople and peasants. If perchance they have spared any suppliants, they have forced them, reduced to the lowest condition of slavery, to fight in the foremost ranks against their own neighbors. . . . They have misused their captives as they have their mares. For they are inhuman and beastly, rather monsters than men, thirsting for and drinking blood, tearing and devouring the flesh of dogs and men, dressed in ox-hides, armed with plates of iron, short and stout, thickset, strong, invincible, indefatigable, their backs unprotected, their breast covered with armor; drinking with delight the pure blood of their flocks, with big, strong horses, which eat branches and even trees. . . . They are without human laws, know no comforts, are more ferocious than lions or bears . . . [and drink] . . . turbid and muddy water when blood fails them [as a beverage]."

The Mongols viciously attack Kiev in 1235.

slashing, destroying, and plundering during the thirteenth century. The Mongols suppressed the Russian people and isolated the nation from foreign contact.

By 1480, the Mongols were gone, but they had influenced Russia in many ways. Copying the Mongol example of autocracy, Russians were ruled by one absolute monarch called a *czar*. Czars held complete, unlimited power over both government and church, claiming their rule was sanctioned by God.

The czar, or emperor, alone made laws, commanded the army and navy, and controlled the Russian Orthodox church. He owned the factories, railroads, schools, and universities. All of life was ruled by him and dictated to the Russian people. The church's role was to reinforce people's obedience to the czar. As historian J.N. Westwood points out, "For ten centuries the Russian Orthodox church was to persuade the people that their suffering under the tsars was good for the soul, and thereby dampened the urge for improvement."[3]

A Small, Privileged Class

The czar, of course, could not manage an empire alone. He had the loyal support of a small class of church officials and landowning nobles. In return, they received important military offices and positions in the government. This small, privileged class exerted great power over the overwhelming majority of Russians.

To the peasants, or serfs, in Russia's largely agrarian economy, the czarist system offered little but misery and oppression. By the nineteenth century, serfs made up more than 80 percent of the population, and few of them owned land. Most of Russia's land, and thus its money, was in the hands of the royal family and other nobles, and the Russian Orthodox church.

For centuries, Russia's serfs, little more than slaves, toiled on Russia's vast farmlands. Fated by birth, serfs legally were bought and sold with the land. They were treated like farm animals—some were even traded for dogs or used as stakes in poker games. Landowners were permitted by law to treat the serfs as property, and many of these workers were beaten and cruelly punished by their owners. Some landowners even used hot irons to brand the faces of disobedient serfs.

Russian nobleman and writer Ivan S. Turgenev wrote that his grandmother once became so enraged by a young serf that she knocked the boy senseless. Next, she put a pillow on his head and sat on it until the youth suffocated. Turgenev reports that his grandmother proclaimed, "Over my subjects I rule as I like and I am not answerable to anyone for them."[4]

Time and time again, serfs rose up against their masters to protest such mistreatment. Some 500 peasant revolts took place between 1825 and 1854. Each time the czar's troops brutally beat the serfs down.

Minorities and Jews Singled Out

Life was little better for Russia's ethnic minorities, the Armenians, the Balts, Estonians, Latvians, Lithuanians, the Poles, and others. They especially resented the czars' ongoing "Russification" effort—they were told to speak only Russian and adopt Russian ways, abandoning their own languages and customs.

Jewish people, who had been persecuted for their religious beliefs throughout Russian history, especially feared the czars. The Jews were often used as scapegoats—wrongly blamed for natural or human-caused calamities. On these occa-

Many religious and ethnic minorities suffered discrimination and persecution in czarist Russia. Russian Jews, especially, were often attacked and killed by czarist troops.

sions, czarist troops launched pogroms (organized attacks) on the Jews. In each pogrom, hundreds of Jews were killed.

Russia Begins to Change

Given the great misery experienced by the majority and the power held by the few, change was bound to come. During wars with France, Russian soldiers were exposed to the ideas of democracy and personal liberty that had sparked democratic revolutions in France and America. Inspired, a group of Russian military officers staged a rebellion against Czar Nicholas I in December 1825, hoping to bring a freer way of life to Russia.

Nicholas, however, ruthlessly crushed the uprising and executed five of the rebel officers. While Nicholas was successful, he

Hoping to topple the repressive czarist regime, Russian officers stage a rebellion against Czar Nicholas I in December 1825. Although unsuccessful, the uprising inspired other Russians to hope for a better life.

To ease growing discontent, Czar Alexander II made significant reforms when he came to power in 1855. Pictured here is the proclamation abolishing serfdom in 1861.

could not crush the hope that the "Decembrists" inspired in the Russian people.

In 1854 Russia again went to war, this time against Britain and France. Russia was defeated, its economy and pride badly affected by the devastating war. The peasants were especially angry: Many had held the mistaken belief that they would be freed after their military service.

When Czar Alexander II came to power in 1855, he knew he could not control the masses of disgruntled serfs. In 1861 he freed 20 million serfs and began a program of land reform. He also eased censorship, created limited local self-governing units, instituted trial by jury, and established new schools and hospitals. Alexander's motives were born of necessity and not humanity: "It is better to do this from above than have it happen from below," he explained.[5]

Alexander's land reform proposals accomplished little. The freed serfs thought they would be given the same plots of land they had tirelessly worked as slaves. Under a complex set of rules, however, peasants generally received only a portion of the land they had worked. They also had to pay their former landlords for the land they did receive. Domestic serfs (household servants) were not allowed to own land at all.

There were other problems. In many cases, land was given not to serfs as individuals, but to a whole village. As the number of people in these villages increased, the share of land each family received became smaller and smaller. Lastly, the land reform rules were so complicated that many freed serfs were cheated out of their land by better educated nobles, who found clever ways of retaining more than half of all Russia's farmlands.

In spite of the mixed success of the land reforms, the freeing of the serfs was one of the most significant events in nineteenth-century Russia. But not for the reasons that Alexander II had hoped. Instead of appeasing the serfs, Alexander's actions increased the peasants' dissatisfaction with his rule. Ultimately, the serfs' long pent-up frustrations would be unleashed, feeding the fires of revolution. Various revolutionary groups began to form to lead the peasants in demanding more than just land—the new aim was a complete end to czarism.

The Czar's Changes Are Not Enough

The first organized revolutionary groups believed that the only way to eliminate czarism was to assassinate the czar. They therefore made many attempts on Alexander's life. In April 1866, for example, a university student fired a pistol at the czar and missed. That same year, while Alexan-
der was traveling in an open carriage in Paris, a woman opened fire at close range. She also missed. Ten years later a gunman unsuccessfully discharged five shots at the czar. In 1879 terrorists blew up the emperor's train. Again Alexander was unhurt. The next year members of a terrorist group calling itself the People's Will bombed the banquet hall of the Winter Palace in St. Petersburg. The czar was untouched.

On March 1, 1881, however, Alexander's luck ran out. The czar was returning from a parade in St. Petersburg when a young man named Nicholas Rysakov tossed a bomb under the royal carriage. The blast killed horses and wounded the royal guards. Shaken but unharmed, Alexander climbed out of the carriage to help the injured men. Just then another assassin, a twenty-five-year-old Polish student, Ignacy Grinevitsky, moved forward. Grinevitsky is said to have yelled, "It is too early to thank God!" before tossing a sec-

Impossible to Stifle Discontent

In Civilization: Past and Present, *the editors quote a message Czar Alexander III received from a terrorist organization.*

"The Government . . . may . . . capture and hang an immense number of separate individuals, it may break up a great number of separate revolutionary groups, it may even destroy the most important of existing revolutionary organizations; but all this will not change, in the slightest degree, the condition of affairs. Revolutionists are the creation of circumstances; of the general discontent of the people; of the striving of Russia after a new social framework . . . it is impossible, by means of repression, to stifle its discontent. Discontent only grows the more when it is repressed."

ond bomb between the czar's feet.

The resulting blast shattered the czar's legs. Mortally wounded, Alexander managed to ask to be brought to the palace.

An hour and a half later, surrounded by priests, doctors, and grief-stricken family members, Alexander II died.

The People's Will released a statement to justify its actions:

> [Alexander] was killed because he did not care for his people. . . . He burdened them with taxes. . . . He cared only for the rich. . . . He himself lived in luxury. . . . He hanged or exiled any who resisted on behalf of the people or on behalf of justice.[6]

The revolutionaries, believing that the death of the czar would lead to democratic reforms in the government, were

Revolutionary groups made many attempts to assassinate Alexander II (above). Finally, on March 1, 1881, a young revolutionary mortally wounded the czar (below). The People's Will stated that Alexander was killed "because he did not care for his people."

During the second half of the nineteenth century, Russia was in the throes of industrialization. This included the construction of the Trans-Siberian Railroad, which connected people from both sides of the huge continent.

encouraged by the assassination. They were wrong: "With the Emperor's assassination," one historian observed, "there died also, for a quarter of a century, any hope that the autocracy might reform itself."[7]

Indeed, the assassination provoked a merciless reaction from the next emperor, Alexander III. During the next thirteen years, the czar's secret police systematically stamped out all signs of unrest or protest.

But this crackdown only increased the Russian people's determination to eliminate the czarist system. Government and military officials would continue to be assassinated by members of an ever-growing number of revolutionary groups.

New Problems Appear

While Russia clung to its unfair and cruel politico-social system, the Industrial Revolution was transforming most countries in western Europe. Powerful, new steam-driven machines, huge factories, and vast amounts of wealth and talent were creating modern, mighty, and prosperous nations.

During the second half of the nineteenth century, Russia, too, began to industrialize rapidly. Superfactories with seemingly endless assembly lines quickly began changing how many people worked and lived. The great Trans-Siberian Railroad was built to join the western reaches of Russia with Vladivostok—a seaport city located thousands of miles away.

From this industrialization process a "working class" developed in Russia. The new industrial laborers, many of them peasants who had left the countryside for the cities, endured virtually intolerable conditions. Factories were often dangerous and dirty. Pay was low and hours were long—often 70 hours or more a week. Even children, some as young as six years of age, worked in dark, polluted factories, often never seeing the sun. Unable to afford even the filthy, crowded workers' dormitories, many people slept beside the machinery. A Russian worker described the deplorable conditions to an English visitor in 1861:

> I earn four roubles [about two dollars] a month. . . . My time is all spent in the [cotton] mill—from five o'clock in the morning until eight o'clock at night. My wife and two daughters work on the field belonging to [a nobleman] five days every week in summer. They get no wages. In winter they do any kind of work required of them by [a supervisor]. My son (who is seventeen years old) works also in the mill and gets two roubles a month.[8]

Such conditions only grew more common as Russia continued to industrialize. An 1881 study of seventy-two factories in Russia revealed that the average worker put in anywhere from 11.50 to 14.25 hours a day. Some worked as long as 20 hours each day.

At the turn of the twentieth century, factory workers in the United States and western Europe faced similar inequities. For them, however, solutions were at least possible. Many U.S. and European workers joined political parties, formed trade unions, and exercised freedom of speech to attempt to bring change to the workplace.

The Horrors of Child Labor

In Albert P. Nenarokov's Russia in the Twentieth Century: The View of a Soviet Historian, *R.V. Gerasimov, a Russian worker turned revolutionary, offers this grisly account of his days as a child laborer in a factory near Narva.*

"Punishment in the factory was meted out by lashing. . . . Once I accidentally broke a broom, which earned me twenty-five lashes, and another time I received fifty lashes for riding the elevator from the fourth to the third floor; they beat me with such force that not a white spot remained on my back; it turned all black. I was sent into the punitive cell on several occasions; in fact, I landed there because I was late for inspection. I will not even bother to talk about the many beatings I received from the foremen and others. . . . All I can say is that at the factory the foremen and assistant foremen were killing children in broad daylight. I was myself witness of a beating which a certain assistant foreman administered to a girl, who died the very following day in the hospital. Children were ordered down on their knees for about two hours where they had to kneel on splinters of old bricks and on rock salt, or were dragged by their hair, whipped with leather straps. . . . In a word, they dealt with them any way they wished."

Workers in a forge in St. Petersburg. The industrial revolution resulted in the creation of a working class, and with it deplorable living and working conditions. These conditions fueled rebelliousness and unrest throughout Russia.

In contrast, most Russian workers had no rights. They also had no legal framework within which to try to alleviate their problems: no congress, parliament, or constitution. Strikes were considered to be a crime against the state and were brutally crushed.

But while Russia's rural poor and working classes had little or no power to alter their lots, Russia's small middle class (bankers, business people, and lawyers) did. They too wished to end, or at least reform, the czarist system. These more fortunate Russians wanted political power and a share in the governing of Russia. They supported governments similar to those in the United States, England, and France. The middle class began to believe that only by creating such a society, based on personal freedoms and democracy, could they obtain their goals. If the middle class could harness and direct the anger of the peasants, an unsuppressible force would form. Russian poet Alexander Blok, writing in 1908, expressed this growing unrest well when he said that a bomb was ticking in the heart of Russia. "Whether we remember or forget, in all of us sit sensations of malaise, fear, catastrophe, explosion."[9] And to make sure that the "bomb" kept on ticking, small groups of Russian radicals instigated a war of ideas.

2 The Seeds of Revolution

"Without a revolutionary theory there can be no revolutionary movement," argued Vladimir Ilyich Lenin, the future leader of the Russian Revolution. Like other Russian intellectuals, Lenin believed that great ideas were the key to achieving great power. And these ideas, once shaped into a theory, could give revolutionaries in Russia the

Russian leader Vladimir Ilyich Lenin believed that "without a revolutionary theory there can be no revolutionary movement."

necessary principles and guidelines to overthrow the czar and create a new society.

During the early nineteenth century, educated Russians were exposed to western European and American ideas. These intellectuals formed a class of people who fervently wanted to solve Russia's massive social, political, and economic problems. Commonly called the intelligentsia, these thinkers eagerly read any writer proposing revolutionary ideas. At first, the group was primarily made up of young nobles who agreed that there must be an end to the wretched poverty, political oppression, and social injustice that plagued Russia. They disagreed, however, over what kind of government should replace the current system and how that change should take place.

During the 1830s and 1840s, the intelligentsia formed into two opposing camps. One of these groups—the "Westerners"—wanted the new Russian society to be heavily inspired by western Europe, with its emphasis on science, constitutional law, and personal freedoms.

The other group, the "Slavophiles," insisted that Russians should ignore the West altogether and focus on developing a system of government that reflected their traditional Slavic culture. Mikhail Mikhailov, a Slavophile writer, said: "We trust in our fresh forces . . . to utter our

The Poor Lot of the Peasant

Alexander Radishchev received a death sentence after penning this sympathetic portrayal of Russia's serfs in A Journey from St. Petersburg to Moscow. *This excerpt is taken from Ian Grey's* History of Russia.

"For the first time I looked closely at all the household gear of a peasant hut. . . . The upper half of the four walls and the whole ceiling were covered with soot; the floor was full of cracks and covered with dirt at least two inches thick. . . . The oven [was] without a smokestack . . . smoke [filled] . . . the hut every morning, winter and summer. . . . Window holes [were covered with] stretched bladders which admitted a dim light at noon time. . . . A trough to feed the pigs and calves [was also in the house]. . . . [The people] sleep together with [the animals], swallowing the air in which a burning candle appears as though shrouded in mist. . . . Here may be seen the greed of [the nobles] . . . and the helplessness of the poor. Ravening beasts, insatiable leeches, what do we leave for the peasants?"

[own] words and not follow in the wake of Europe."[10]

The Slavophiles opposed serfdom, but they favored retaining the Russian Orthodox church and the czar as Russia's highest authorities. Slavophiles believed that by sticking to traditional Slavic society, they could achieve on a national level the same sense of community that had existed in the peasant villages. This would more fit the Russian personality, Slavophiles believed, than would the harsh individualism emphasized in western Europe.

Alexander Herzen, a leading radical author in the 1830s and 1840s, who influenced many revolutionaries, issued the following warning:

Russia's future will be a great danger for Europe and a great misfortune for Russia if there is no emancipation of the individual. One more century of present despotism [autocracy] will destroy all the good qualities of the Russian people.[11]

The best solution for the peasants, according to Herzen, was to develop the Slavophile ideals into a form of *socialism*—the system under which government exerts great control of the economy for the benefit of all. Herzen's teachings led to a movement called *populism*, which theorized that adhering to the traditional peasant life would lead to modern socialism. The populist theory also advocated revolution from below—the peasants were the ones who should start and drive the czar's overthrow.

Beginning in the 1840s, the populist movement gained members as a new gen-

Author Alexander Herzen was an early advocate of socialism. His teachings led to the populist movement, which gained support into the 1870s.

eration of non-nobles joined. They were the sons and daughters of the middle class—government workers, business executives, the clergy.

Continuing into the 1870s, revolutionary-minded university students were so taken by the idea of bringing the populist message "to the people" that they dressed as peasants and fanned out across the Russian countryside, trying to stir up revolutionary feelings among the former serfs. But Russia's peasants were hard to convince. Although most of them desperately wanted land reform and a better way of life, a great many still had respect, even adoration, for the czar. Their anger was fo-

cused on the czar's government officials, not the monarch himself. Thus, many peasants received the revolutionaries' urgings with indifference, suspicion, and sometimes even violence.

Terrorism and Assassinations Begin

The failure to incite or even to intrigue the peasants with populism led to its decline. The ideas of another influential intellectual, Mikhail Bakunin, a member of Russia's nobility and a former artillery officer, gained influence. In his book *God and the State*, Bakunin demanded anarchy—no government at all. As the first step to this goal, Russia would have to get rid of its hated ruling class. And to this end, Bakunin urged revolutionaries to use terrorism. As he stated: "Our first work must be the annihilation of everything as it now exists."[12]

Bakunin-inspired *terrorist cells*, secret groups of activists, developed across Russia. Destruction, not reform, was their goal. One of them wrote: "What can be smashed must be smashed. Whatever will stand the blow is sound, what flies into smithereens is rubbish."[13]

Added Sergei Genadyevich Nechayev, another Russian revolutionary: "Night and day [the revolutionist] must have but one thought, one aim—merciless destruction."[14]

This faith in destruction as a means of improving Russia found ultimate expression in a movement called *nihilism*, which developed in the 1860s. According to the novelist Turgenev, a nihilist "is a man who does not bow to any authorities, who does not take any principle on trust, no matter with what respect that principle is surrounded."[15]

During the 1870s, nihilists began terrorizing Russian government officials by bombing government buildings and attempting assassinations. One of the most notorious of these groups was the People's Will—the underground organization that had assassinated Czar Alexander II.

By now, some intellectuals believed that the peasants were too ignorant to grasp radical ideas and unwilling to lead a revolution in any event. Thus, they argued, what the revolution now needed was a series of cadres, tight-knit groups of competent activists who would provide leadership and discipline to carry out a revolution.

One intellectual, Peter Tkachev, helped develop the concept for the kind of revolutionary party that would later emerge:

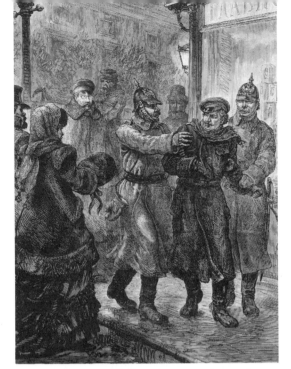

Officials detain a nihilist after a terrorist attack. Nihilists questioned authority and advocated destruction of political institutions.

Mikhail Bakunin founded a movement of political anarchism. He urged revolutionaries to use terrorism to achieve their goals.

On the banner of the revolutionary party, a party of action rather than a party of reasoning, may be inscribed only the following words: struggle against the government, struggle against the existing order of things, struggle to the last drop of blood—to the last breath.[16]

In fact, argued another leading writer, Nicholas Gavrilovich Chernyshevsky, a new ruthless breed of individual—a "new man"—was needed to make the revolution succeed. Chernyshevsky's book, *What Is to Be Done?*, spelled out a vision of the new revolutionary and became what one reviewer called "the literary Bible of two generations of revolutionaries."[17]

A future Russia, wrote Chernyshevsky, would be led by "strong personalities, who

Leading writer Nicholas Gavrilovich Chernyshevsky wrote the influential What Is to Be Done?, *often dubbed the "revolutionary's bible."*

[would] impose their character on the pattern of events and hurry their course, who [would] give a direction to the chaotic upheaval of forces [already] taking place in the movement of the masses."[18]

Adding to this ferment of ideas were the writings of Karl Marx, the German political philosopher and father of modern socialism. Like so many other educated people during the nineteenth century, Marx had been dismayed by the inhumane conditions endured by the European working classes. Marx argued that the industrial workers, or "proletarians," were no less trapped than the slaves of earlier times; the enslavement of the workers, however, was not as obvious. Yes, workers were free to quit their low-paying jobs, which barely kept them from starvation. But they were doomed to go to another factory that paid similar starvation wages. They could never start their own factories, because the

tools—that is, the means of production—were too big and too costly for workers to hope to own. Only those with money and power, Marx pointed out, could afford to acquire and control the means of production. And in most industrialized countries money and power were largely in the hands of the middle class, or bourgeoisie.

Along with the bourgeoisie, workers had another enemy, Marx argued—organized religion. By promising a better life in heaven, the church, said Marx, conspired to keep poor, uneducated industrial workers content with horrid circumstances on earth.

Through his writings such as *The Communist Manifesto*, which he coauthored with Friedrich Engels, and *Das Kapital* (or

The German philosopher Karl Marx, whose important socialist philosophy shaped the revolutionary movement. Marx is often called the father of modern socialism.

"Working Men Unite"

Karl Marx and Friedrich Engels's Communist Manifesto, *a pamphlet that changed the course of history, begins with the following famous words.*

"A spectre is haunting Europe—the spectre of communism. All the powers of old Europe have entered into a holy alliance to exorcise this spectre; Pope and Czar, Metternich and Guizot [nineteenth-century statesmen representing Austria and France, respectively], French Radicals and German police-spies. . . .

Two things result from this fact:

1. Communism is already acknowledged by all European powers to be itself a power.
2. It is high time that Communists should openly, in the face of the world, publish their views, their aims, their tendencies . . . with a manifest of the party itself. . . .

The history of all hitherto existing society is the history of class struggles.

Freeman and slave, patrician and plebeian, lord and serf, guild-master and journeyman, in a word, oppressor and oppressed, stood in constant opposition to one another, carried on an uninterrupted, now hidden, now open fight, a fight that each time ended either in a revolutionary reconstitution of society at large, or in the common ruin of the contending classes. . . .

[In our own time] . . . society . . . [has split] into great hostile camps, into two great classes directly facing each other: Bourgeoisie and Proletariat.

The Communists . . . openly declare that their ends can be attained only by the forcible overthrow of all existing social conditions. Let the ruling classes tremble at a Communist revolution. The proletarians have nothing to lose but their chains. They have a world to win.

Working men of all countries, unite."

Capital, as in "capitalism"), Marx explained that revolution was inevitable. Throughout history, he said, societies around the world underwent a series of armed struggles between opposing social classes of people—those who had power and wealth, and those who did not. At the end of each cycle, either the opposing classes had destroyed themselves or a new society had been produced, reflecting revolutionary changes.

Marx predicted a final class struggle, in which factory workers would rise up against the middle-class owners of industry to destroy capitalism (an economic system based on private ownership of businesses and industries). As a result, the workers, as a group, would come to own and operate the factories and businesses themselves. In this new "communist" state, workers would contribute to society according to their capabilities, and they would take from society what they needed to survive. Marx believed that violent revolution would be necessary to bring about this state of affairs, because he thought it would be impossible for the workers to persuade the middle class to share the wealth and power. Marx wrote that "The point is not to understand the world, but to change it."[19]

Marx's ideas contrasted sharply with other revolutionary ideas, even those that also advocated violence. Just as earlier intellectuals had doubted the peasants' capacity for effective revolutionary action, many Marxists viewed other revolutionary groups' terrorist acts as both pointless and wasteful. It was much better, they argued, to develop hardened radical cadres to lead the country into revolution. All followers should be prepared to carry out orders unquestioningly from this decision-making elite.

As suggested above, Marxists neither expected nor wanted Russia's peasants to be the vanguard of the revolution. Marxists believed the front-line position was meant for the industrial workers of the cities—the proletarians.

Marxism, nihilism, populism—these movements and so many other radical belief systems transformed educated Russian youth of the late nineteenth century into a revolutionary generation.

What was needed next to put revolutionary thought into powerful action was leadership. In 1887 that leadership was brought to the forefront of the revolutionary movement.

Lenin Emerges

On May 8, 1887, five university students were hanged for planning to kill Czar Alexander III. Among those executed was a mild, well-brought-up, middle-class youth named Alexander Ilyich Ulyanov. His death

Lenin at the age of twenty-two. The young Lenin vowed to abolish the repressive czarist system after his brother was executed for participating in a plot to assassinate Alexander III.

The Life of the Young Revolutionary

The passion for self-sacrifice, violence, and radicalism which gripped so many of Russia's young revolutionaries, is dramatized in this famous passage from Turgenev's novel The Threshold, *quoted by Alan Moorehead in* The Russian Revolution.

"To you who desire to cross this threshold, do you know what awaits you?"

"I know," replied the girl.

"Cold, hunger, abhorrence, derision, contempt, abuse, prison, disease, and death!"

"I know, I am ready, I shall endure all blows."

"Not from enemies alone, but also from relatives, from friends."

"Yes, even from them . . ."

"Are you ready to commit a crime?"

"I am ready for crime too."

"Do you know that you may be disillusioned in that which you believe, that you may discover that you were mistaken, that you ruined your life in vain?"

"I know that too."

"Enter!"

The girl crossed the threshold and a heavy curtain fell behind her. Fool! said someone gnashing his teeth. Saint! someone uttered in reply.

might have been just another forgotten drop in the sea of blood of the millions of Russians who would die violently in the coming decades. But Alexander's grief-stricken younger brother Vladimir became obsessed with hate for the czar who had ordered his sibling's execution. Upon Alexander's death, seventeen-year-old Vladimir wailed, "I'll make them pay for this! I swear it!"[20]

It was a vow he would fulfill. One day, the entire world would know this younger Ulyanov brother as Lenin—one of history's greatest political leaders and the architect of the Russian Revolution. The early days of Vladimir Ulyanov scarcely hinted at the radicalism for which V.I. Lenin became famous. A red-haired youth with distinctive high cheekbones and slanting Tatar eyes, Lenin was born in 1870 at Simbirsk, located on the Volga River. His father, Ilya Ulyanov, a school inspector, was loyal to the czar and devoted to the Russian Orthodox church. Lenin's mother, a school teacher, was a physician's daughter.

Lenin enjoyed a comfortable childhood with his three sisters and two brothers. He particularly adored Alexander, whom the family called Sasha. When Alexander was arrested for taking part in the assassination of the czar, Ilya Ulyanov was dead. This left only Ulyanov's widow to try her best to help her son defend himself at the trial. No one in town would assist her in any way, including her numerous liberal friends. The callous treatment of his mother created in Lenin a deep and lasting dislike of bourgeois hypocrisy.

Because of Alexander's conviction, Lenin was not allowed to enter the university his older brother had attended. Instead, he studied law at the University of Kazan, where he ran afoul of local authorities for participating in student protests.

During the next several years, influenced by many radical authors, Lenin transformed himself into a hard-core revolutionary. For example, Peter Tkachev's writing convinced Lenin of the need for a highly disciplined political party, ruthless enough to do whatever was necessary to topple the czarist system.

After reading Chernyshevsky's *What Is to Be Done?*, Lenin became convinced that he was one of those "strong personalities" destined to lead a new Russia. For the rest of his life, Lenin would cherish Chernyshevsky's book, berating anyone who dared to disagree with his high opinion of this "revolutionary's bible."

The writings of Karl Marx most heavily influenced Lenin. Here, thought Lenin, was the blueprint for revolution he had been seeking. Marx's work combined the call for action with a plan based on theory. Workers in Russia, Lenin observed, faced the same squalid conditions described by Marx. Although the German theorist expected a communist revolution to take place in a highly industrialized country, Lenin came to believe that Marxism could be employed to transform his native country, backward and still mostly rural though it was.

Lenin, along with like-minded individuals, spent his days and nights writing radical articles and pamphlets and calling for

Gripped by an intense desire to create a new Russia, Lenin (center) transformed himself into a hard-core revolutionary and surrounded himself with like-minded individuals.

Opposed to political terrorism, Georgi Plekhanov espoused Menshevik views in contrast to Lenin, who headed the radical Bolsheviks.

a Marxist revolution in Russia. These activities resulted in his arrest, and in 1895 he was exiled to Siberia for four years. Ironically, the punishment put Lenin in touch with fellow exiled intellectuals, with whom he shared ideas. While in Siberia, he married a fellow exiled radical, Nadezhda K. Krupskaya, a young school teacher.

After their release, Lenin and Krupskaya wandered western Europe together, meeting other Marxists from many countries, writing, arguing, organizing, and preparing for revolution. For a while, they settled in Munich, where Lenin edited *Iskra* (*The Spark*), a radical publication that had to be smuggled into Russia.

During the early days of the Russian Marxist movement, a wide spectrum of opinion developed over how Marx's ideas could, and should, be put into action. The year 1898 saw the formation of a new political party, the Russian Social Democratic Labor party. Led by Georgi Plekhanov, a pioneer of Marxism in Russia, the Social Democrats (SDs), attempted to find common ground for the followers of Marx. By 1903, though, bickering had caused the organization to split into two groups: the "Bolsheviks" (the majority), and the "Mensheviks" (the minority).

Social change, argued the Mensheviks, should come slowly and democratically. And the movement should be open to anybody who was sympathetic to Marxism. The Bolsheviks, now headed by Lenin, wanted to seize power by violent, nondemocratic means. The coming revolution, they insisted, should be led by a handful of committed radicals, not a group whose membership was open to anyone.

While the Marxists bickered, another revolutionary group was fast making headway in Russia: the Socialist Revolutionaries (SRs). This group would soon be a major rival to the Marxists. To some degree, the SRs were a modern remake of the populist movement. They viewed the peasants as the backbone of a popular uprising against the czar, favored socialism and democracy, and did not mind using terrorism.

As Lenin and other radicals debated the theory of revolution in exile, Russia was reeling under the incompetent and harsh reactionary ways of another emperor, Nicholas II—the last of the Romanov czars.

Revolution was beginning to rumble at last.

3 Taking It to the Streets: The First Revolution

Upon the death of his father, Alexander III, Nicholas Romanov, became Czar Nicholas II at age twenty-six. Elegant, handsome, dashing, and charming, he seemed the ideal candidate to play the role. As Count Grabbe, a high-ranking general close to the royal family observed, "Time and again, I was witness to the fact

Nicholas Romanov became czar of Russia upon the death of his father Alexander III. Although charming and dashing, Nicholas II was not a skillful politician.

that even persons ill disposed politically came away from an audience with [Nicholas] under the spell of his personality."[21]

Despite these qualities, Nicholas soon demonstrated that he was not cut out to be an autocrat. Unlike his father, Nicholas was not decisive and assertive. He avoided arguments and confrontations. He did not seem very interested in the problems of his people or the affairs of government. "I know absolutely nothing about matters of state," Nicholas revealed on the day he became czar.[22]

In *The History of the Russian Revolution*, Leon Trotsky, a major actor in the events of the time and an enemy of the czar, offered an opinion of Nicholas that was echoed by many:

> Nicholas was not only unstable, but treacherous. Flatterers called him a charmer, bewitcher, because of his gentle way with the courtiers. But the tzar reserved his special caresses for just those officials who he had decided to dismiss. . . . [He] felt at ease only among completely mediocre and brainless people . . . to whom he did not have to look up.[23]

Nicholas's decision to wed Princess Alexandra of Hesse-Darmstadt just a few

Nicholas's marriage to Princess Alexandra disquieted many Russians, who viewed the new empress as overbearing and autocratic.

weeks after his father's death did nothing to increase his popularity. A pretty young woman who had been born in Germany and reared in England, Alexandra was also a granddaughter of Britain's Queen Victoria. Because the czar's new wife was foreign born, many Russians assumed (incorrectly) that she was passionately pro-German. Moreover, Alexandra spoke no Russian and belonged to the Church of England, not the Russian Orthodox church. Also of great concern to Russians in the years to come was her ability to dominate her weaker-willed husband.

"By nature high-strung, timid, and secretive, she was judged by some in Russia to be cold and unfriendly," writes Grabbe.[24] Trotsky is even harsher in his assessment of Alexandra: "This Hessian princess was literally possessed by the demon of autocracy. . . . [She] supplemented the weak-willed tzar, ruling over him. . . . Even more than he, she craved the society of simpletons."[25]

The Czar's Troubles Begin Early

Nicholas's reign seemed to be jinxed from its onset. During his coronation ceremony in Moscow, the old capital of Russia, a St. Andrew's cross Nicholas had been wearing fell to his feet. Many observers interpreted the accident as an omen of bad times to come.

Later the same day, the royal couple made a huge mistake in judgment that would darken their reputation forever. For several days, immense crowds of Russia's poor—perhaps 600,000 strong—had been gathering on the Khodynka Field outside Moscow to take part in the festivities honoring Nicholas. In accordance with tradition, they were to receive humble gifts from their new ruler. When a false rumor swept through the crowd that there were not enough gifts to go around, people panicked. They began pushing and shoving. Soon a human stampede was under way. By the end of the day, 1,300 men, women, and children were dead.

Nicholas and Alexandra, as if unconcerned with the horror that had taken place on the field, proceeded to the French ambassador's ball, elsewhere in the city. The Russian people were shocked and angered by what they saw as insensitivity and indifference to a great tragedy. Revolutionaries now added another grievance to their list of hatreds of czarist rule.

Crop failures at the turn of the century resulted in widespread famine. Desperate for food and work, Russian peasants fled to the cities.

The First Revolt Begins

By the dawning of the twentieth century, Russia's industrialization was near completion. Many factories had been built and capital from foreign investors poured into the country. This industrialization, however, was made at the expense of the masses. Nicholas had decided to plow the nation's resources into the industrialization effort, rather than upgrading the standards of living of the poor. Thus the quality of life for Russia's multitudes did not improve. In fact, workers and peasants were losing ground. In addition, crop failures in 1897, 1898, and 1901 resulted in widespread famine and sent desperate peasants fleeing to the cities to look for food and work.

During 1901 and 1902, peasant uprisings occurred in Kharov and Poltava provinces. The cry was heard across Russia for more farmland for the peasants, and fewer taxes. Meanwhile, several cities experienced massive strikes, work stoppages, and protest demonstrations by industrial workers.

Russia's revolutionary groups were behind much of the growing unrest. The Social Democrats fanned the fires of protest with Marxist propaganda, and the Socialist Revolutionaries (SRs) continued to assassinate government officials and incite peasants to burn their masters' manor homes.

Nicholas punished rioters and protesters severely. Indeed, his reactions to these uprisings were the only consistent, decisive responses he made during his troubled rule. In 1900 alone, the Russian police arrested 1,580 people for political crimes. By 1903, 5,590 had been arrested. These figures are consistent with the czar's vow to "maintain the principle of autocracy just as firmly and unflinchingly as it was preserved by my unforgettable dead father."[26]

In February 1904, with the power struggle between the workers and the czar at a standstill, war broke out between Russia and Japan. The czar saw the war as an opportunity to distract Russia's workers from revolutionary ideas, uniting them in the goal of fighting a common enemy. The war might also allow Russia to expand its power and influence.

Trouble had been brewing between Japan and Russia for some time. Much of the feud centered on a treaty Russia had negotiated with China, which allowed Russia access to the Chinese seaports of Dairen and Port Arthur. The treaty also permitted Russia to build a railroad through Manchuria to get to these ports. Japanese leaders, however, worried that Russia har-

bored secret plans to take control of both Manchuria and nearby Korea—an area Japan was also interested in dominating.

For several weeks, Russia and Japan attempted to solve their dispute diplomatically. The war began when the Japanese, without warning, launched a naval attack against the Russians at Port Arthur.

From the beginning, Russia was at a disadvantage, and at the end of the 18-month war, Japan was a clear victor. Russia had suffered a series of humiliating military defeats, with casualties mounting as Japan's modern warships destroyed the czar's aging fleet.

At the start of the war, Russians from all levels of society rallied around the czar. But as news of military disaster and thousands of deaths began to filter back, popular support turned to outrage. Antiwar protests began to materialize. The ever-violent SRs continued to riot in the streets, trying to take full advantage of the public's anger.

To counter these problems, the czar relied on the advice of Vyacheslav K. Plehve, his minister of internal affairs. Years

Hand-to-hand struggle during the war with Japan in 1904. Unsupportive of the war, outraged Russians joined forces in opposing the government.

A Preference for Death

The Russian Revolution by Lionel Kochan includes a translation of the petition that was intended for delivery to Czar Nicholas on "Bloody Sunday."

"O Sire, . . . we working men of St. Petersburg, our wives and children, and our parents, helpless and aged men and women, have come to you, our ruler, in quest of justice and protection. We are beggars, we are oppressed and overburdened with work; we are insulted, we are not regarded as human beings but are treated as slaves who must suffer their bitter lot in silence. We have suffered but are driven further and further into the abyss of poverty, injustice, and ignorance; we are strangled by despotism and tyranny, so that we can breathe no longer. We have no strength at all, O Sovereign. Our patience is at an end. We are approaching that terrible moment when death is better than the continuance of intolerable sufferings."

before, Plehve had assisted in capturing the conspirators responsible for the assassination of Alexander II. Nicholas hoped for the same sort of success now in quelling the outrage of the public, and indeed, Plehve mounted a ruthless, somewhat successful, campaign against all suspected enemies of the czar. In July 1904, however, Plehve was killed by a terrorist's bomb.

Bloody Sunday

Against this backdrop of violence and unrest, another event sparked the inevitable march toward revolution. A Russian Orthodox priest named Georgy A. Gapon, a tall, somber, dark-bearded man of peasant stock, had secretly agreed with the St. Petersburg city police to organize industrial workers. At the time, the police were convinced that by setting up trade unions, they would be able to influence, if not manipulate, troublesome workers.

The police, however, greatly underestimated Father Gapon. They also failed to realize the extent of the priest's proletarian sympathies. Setting aside his role as secret agent, the clergyman became a real labor leader. When workers were fired from the Putilov machine and engine factory—one of the biggest such plants in the world—Gapon called for a strike. Within a week, 100,000 disgruntled workers had walked off the job.

On the chilly morning of January 22, 1905, the priest led a crowd of some 200,000 men, women, and children through the snow-covered streets of St. Petersburg, to the Winter Palace. Hungry, oppressed, and dispirited, the marchers were taking their case directly to the czar. Gapon believed that if the people appealed to the czar himself, they would receive a compassionate response. Those who marched with Gapon agreed; they were still loyal to their emperor, despite his weaknesses. They blamed the government, not Nicholas, for their misery.

The demonstrators carried religious pictures of the czar and sang patriotic songs as they marched. They also bore a petition demanding an end to the war and civil rights for all Russians. One worker cried out to the crowd:

> You know why we are going. We are going to the czar for the Truth. Our life is beyond endurance. . . . Now we must save Russia from the bureaucrats under whose weight we suffer. They squeeze the sweat and blood out of us. You know our workers' life. We live ten families to the room. . . . And so we go to the czar. If he is our czar, if he loves his people he must listen to us. . . . We go to him with open hearts. . . . It cannot be that he would fire on us.[27]

As the throngs of mostly peaceful and orderly marchers neared the Winter Palace, the Cossack guards (Russia's elite mounted troops) waited for them. The Cossacks ordered the crowd to disperse, but Gapon's demonstrators held their ground. Soldiers on horseback, armed with whips and sabers, charged the protesters. Still, the crowd would not disperse. Suddenly, soldiers began firing on men, women, and children. Within minutes, some 300 unarmed demonstrators lay dead in the blood-stained snow; another 700 were wounded.

"A terrible day," Nicholas confided to his diary later that day. "Troops had to fire in many places of the city, and there were many killed or wounded. God, how painful and awful."[28]

The czar's grief was not widely conveyed to the public, however. In fact, the czar refused to criticize the army for opening fire on the protesters. Instead, he decided to meet a group of workers at another of his palaces, Tsarskoe Selo. Here he served the workers tea, scolded them, and advised them to ignore the revolutionaries.

"Bloody Sunday," as this day would be remembered, became a revolutionary battle cry across the country. Riots, mutinies, terrorist attacks, peasant uprisings, and strikes burst across the empire. For the first time, a genuine wave of revolution

Georgy A. Gapon set up an association of industrial workers to deal with grievances. Strongly sympathetic to the proletariat, he led demonstrators in an appeal to the czar.

shook the nation. Workers angrily demanded 8-hour days, a democratic government, and freedom for political prisoners. Even areas outside Russia but under its control such as Poland, the Baltic states of Lithuania, Latvia, and Estonia, and the Caucasus areas were calling for freedom from czarist rule.

One of the new voices calling for open revolt was that of Father Gapon. Having lost all faith in the czar, he became a confirmed revolutionary. In a public letter he raged against

> Nicholas Romanov, formerly Tsar and at present soul-murderer of the Russian empire. The innocent blood of workers, their wives and children lies forever between you and the Russian people. . . . May all the blood which must be spilled fall upon you, you Hangman! I call upon all the socialist parties of Russia to come to an immediate agreement among themselves and begin an armed uprising against Tsarism.[29]

Unfortunately for Gapon, other revolutionaries remained skeptical about the sincerity of his radical sentiments. The Socialist Revolutionaries, in fact, believed he was still a police agent and lynched him.

Fearful of being killed themselves, the czar and his family fled St. Petersburg and cruised off the Baltic coast in the royal yacht, waiting for the violence to subside.

Nicholas Permits the Duma

Shaken by the violence wracking his nation, Nicholas hastily promised that he would give in to one of the most popular of the workers' demands. That is, he agreed to allow the creation of an "Imperial Duma"—a sort of Russian congress with elected delegates. At first, many Russians greeted this announcement with satisfaction. But in August 1905 when the government revealed the details of the czar's proposals, the popular mood quickly

Soldiers open fire on peaceful, unarmed protesters near the Winter Palace. In the wake of "Bloody Sunday," widespread disorder and open revolt shook the country.

soured. The people learned, for example, that seats in the Duma were to be filled only by members of the nobility and the middle class, and peasants who were loyal to the zemstvos—small local self-governing units. Russia's industrial workers and ethnic minorities would not be represented. Even worse, the Duma would have no independent law-making power. Real authority remained with the czar.

Once more Russians reacted. Streets swelled with demonstrators. Across Russia the biggest strike in history began shutting down factories, hospitals, newspapers, and businesses. By October 1905, the country was paralyzed.

During this chaos, the seeds of an alternative government were sprouting across Russia. Various "*soviets*" or councils, began to appear, and they gave instructions and weapons to others to lead and fuel the uprisings.

The most successful of them all was the St. Petersburg Soviet, with some 500 delegates. It represented about 250,000 workers. Begun by the Mensheviks and others, the St. Petersburg Soviet not only provided a forum for parliamentary-style debates among its worker-delegates, but also put out its own newspaper and formed its own militia.

Foremost among the leaders of the St. Petersburg Soviet was a brilliant twenty-six-year-old former university math student and free-lance journalist named Lev D. Bronstein, whose revolutionary name was Leon Trotsky. A diehard Marxist from his university days, Trotsky had spent many years in exile. But when revolution erupted in 1905, he returned to Russia to fight with the Mensheviks. Twelve years later, he would become one of the most powerful of all the Russian revolutionaries.

Lenin, too, was hard at work during this time. From the safety of Geneva, Switzerland, where many exiled Russians now resided, Lenin sent advice to fellow revolutionaries: "It horrifies me—I give you my word, to find there has been talk about bombs for over six months, yet not one has been made. . . . Form fighting squads at once everywhere."[30]

During the disorder, Czar Nicholas floundered. His prime minister, Count Witte, pointed out that there were only two ways to save the empire: declare a military dictatorship and brutally restore

A rising wave of strikes and riots paralyzed the country by October 1905. Here, students demonstrate in St. Petersburg.

order, or allow real and meaningful reform, leading to democratic government.

Nicholas first asked his second cousin, the grand duke Nicholas Niklayevich, to become a military dictator. Niklayevich not only refused but vowed to shoot himself unless Nicholas set up a duma, saying, "It is necessary for the good of Russia, and all of us."[31]

Nicholas had no other option. On October 30, 1905, he reluctantly made what he later called a terrible decision: he released the "October Manifesto." This decree allowed the creation of a constitutional monarchy, including an elected duma. This meant that although the monarchy would still exist, it would be governed by the rules and laws of the

Prologue to Revolution

Leon Trotsky, in The History of the Russian Revolution, *describes the turbulent events of 1905.*

"The events of 1905 were a prologue to the two revolutions of 1917, that of February and that of October. In the prologue all the elements of the drama were included, but not carried through. The Russo-Japanese war made tzarism totter. . . . The liberal bourgeoisie [middle class] had frightened the monarchy. . . . Peasant uprisings to seize the land occurred throughout vast stretches of the country. . . . The revolutionary parts of the army tended toward the soviets, which at the moment of highest tension openly disputed the power with the monarch. . . . However, all the revolutionary forces were then going into action for the first time, lacking experience and confidence. . . . Although with a few broken ribs, tzarism came out of the experience of 1905 alive and strong enough."

Leon Trotsky, one of the most powerful of all revolutionaries.

Debris litters a street in Kronstadt after an uprising in October 1905.

Duma. The manifesto also permitted more civil liberties. Supreme power, however, remained in the hands of the czar. At first, newly created political parties, such as the liberal "Kadets" and the moderately conservative "Octobrists," appeared to be content with the new system of government.

But Russia's radical political groups were far from happy. At the other end of the spectrum, extreme conservative factions who still favored absolute autocracy were outraged. Some of them vented their rage by launching pogroms against Russia's traditional scapegoats—the Jews.

Russia's leftist revolutionary groups were caught off guard by the czar's change of heart. They were also unimpressed. As Trotsky wrote, "The proletariat knows what it does and does not want. . . . It rejects the police whip wrapped in the parchment of the constitution."[32]

Lenin hurried to St. Petersburg in November 1905 to help his revolutionary followers form a strategy in response to the czar's actions. But he was too late. The momentum of the revolution was fading fast. The czar's moves, while not going as far as the radicals wanted, did satisfy enough Russians to weaken opposition to the czar. The Imperial troops also managed to suppress all major uprisings by the end of 1905.

On July 21, 1906, representatives to the Duma met for the first time in St. Petersburg. Here, they made clear that they intended to exert real law-making power. They called for meaningful political reform and demanded an accounting for the war with Japan. Nicholas responded the next month by dissolving the Duma and setting up new election laws which, in effect, reduced opposition to the czar by decreasing the number of non-Russians or peoples living in territories ruled by Russia, peasants, and workers who could be elected. New elections were duly held, and the Duma met again in September, this

Although Prime Minister Stolypin instituted massive land reform plans, he also ruthlessly suppressed opposition to the czar.

time composed of greater numbers of large landowners and members of the wealthy middle class, who were more likely to agree with the czar and his advisers.

Although Nicholas seemed to be subverting true reform, his advisers continued to recommend further change, knowing that for Russia to succeed economically, agriculture would have to be less wasteful and inefficient. Nicholas's newest prime minister, P.A. Stolypin, recommended more individually owned farms. Stolypin launched a massive land reform plan that included cheap loans and technical assistance to peasants.

Unfortunately, the president of the Duma was also assigned the task of eliminating opposition to the czar. This job was difficult. By 1906, radicals had killed 1,400 people. That figure would grow to 3,000 in 1907. Under Stolypin's command, police troops began ruthlessly snuffing out uprisings everywhere. Terrorists, reformers, peasants, workers—everyone, it now seemed—became a target for government bullets and swords. Village after village was shot up and burned as the czar's troops inflicted their terrible punishment. Across Russia, "Stolypin's necktie" (a bitter nickname for the hangman's noose) executed thousands. Stolypin's violent oppression led to his death by an assassin's bullet in September 1911.

Stolypin's assassination did nothing to quell the violence and terror that continued to plague Russia. What saved the czarist government, at least temporarily, was the outbreak of yet another war.

4 The Great War and the Mad Monk

In early 1914 Europe was ripe for war. Nations were divided into hostile camps, armed, and spoiling for conflict. For decades, they had ruthlessly competed against one another for colonies and natural resources around the world. Ever suspicious, they made military alliances with other countries for protection.

All that was needed to inflame the continent was a spark. It finally came one hot summer morning. On June 28, 1914, in the city of Sarajevo, which was then part of Austria, a gunman shot and killed Archduke Francis Ferdinand, the heir to the throne of the Austrian empire.

Immediately, Austrian officials accused nearby Serbia of involvement in the assassination plot and threatened war. Almost simultaneously, Russia began to mobilize in support of Serbia, its Slavic ally. Next, Germany, which had pledged to defend Austria, declared war on Russia and

Archduke Francis Ferdinand minutes before his assassination on June 28, 1914. His death signaled the advent of World War I.

Russian and Hungarian soldiers during World War I. More than 15 million Russians were called to arms. Russia's military, however, was poorly trained and under the command of ineffective leaders.

France. Despite the best efforts of diplomats to avoid violence, some 27 countries entered the fray. World War I had begun.

The Russian people again rallied around the czar. Historian Bernard Pares noted the sudden outburst of patriotism: "The vast multitude fell upon their knees and sang 'God Save the Tsar' as it had never been sung before."[33]

In this spirit of national unity, Czar Nicholas could not have been more agreeable to the elected legislators of his country. He wrote to the president of the Duma, which had just voted on funding for the war, "I am your friend until death. I will do anything for the Duma. Tell me what you want."[34]

In a fever of nationalism, Russian patriots attacked the German embassy in St. Petersburg, a city whose German name was changed to something more Russian-sounding—Petrograd. The public also turned against Lenin's Bolsheviks, who were protesting Russia's involvement in the war. Revolution, for the moment, was largely forgotten by the common people.

A Disaster for Russia

More than 15 million Russian men were called to military duty. At first, England and France, Russia's allies in western Europe, had hoped the "Russian steamroller" would help them overwhelm the Germans. The Russians were successful in an early attack against the Austrians in the enemy's province of Galicia. But, they suffered a major defeat in Tannenberg, Germany. Not long after, the Germans dealt them a catastrophic blow in the battle of the Masurian Lakes, forcing the czar's troops out of German territory.

Russia's allies soon lost faith in the Russian army, which included legions of poorly disciplined, uneducated peasants. Within the next three years, between 6 and 8 million of these recruits would become casualties: dead, wounded, or missing.

Russia simply was not prepared for modern war. Its army was poorly trained, its weaponry and military methods old-fashioned, and many of its leaders incompetent or corrupt. Semi-industrialized, Russia also lacked the resources to sustain a major military effort. Food, equipment, and clothing were constantly in short supply. Many soldiers went barefoot into battle. While most modern armies in Europe wore steel helmets, Russia's soldiers wore visored cloth caps; even worse, some 25 percent of them were ordered into combat without weapons.

Against the powerful German troops, the ill-equipped Russians were a poor match. Russian officers also stubbornly re-fused to accommodate their battle plans to modern German ordnance, which included the machine gun, a rapid-firing automatic weapon. They insisted, as well, on observing an outdated, and suicidal, tradition that prevented Russian officers from crawling on the battlefield. During 1914, the first year of fighting, Russian losses were appalling: almost 4 million were killed. One German field commander complained that it was difficult for his troops to use their machine guns because there were so many Russian corpses on the battlefields.

By 1915, German troops occupied much of the western territories of the Russian empire and were advancing eastward toward Moscow. As the Germans proceeded, Russian generals ordered their troops to retreat and begin a scorched-earth action, to deny the invaders the booty of war. Soldiers burned peasant farms, homes, and crops and destroyed bridges and roads.

As a result of these destructive acts, mobs of frightened refugees fled the be-

Russian corpses blanket a battlefield in 1915. Russian losses were so devastating that one German officer remarked that his troops had difficulty using their machine guns because so many corpses littered the battlefield.

A Flood of Humanity

E.M. Halliday's Russia in Revolution *contains an excerpt of a government report from the czar's council of ministers which gives a glimpse of Russian refugees fleeing the eastern front of World War I.*

"The immense stream of uprooted, desperate, suffering humanity rolls along the roads interfering with military traffic and completely disorganizing the rear of the army. . . . Men and women die by the hundreds from hunger, exposure, and disease. The death rate among the children has reached a terrible height. Unburied corpses are left along the roads. The decaying carcasses of dead animals poison the atmosphere. And this flood of humanity spreads over all Russia, adds to war-time hardships, creates a shortage of foodstuffs, increases the cost of living, and accentuates the discontent which is nowhere lacking."

sieged areas and began clogging the streets of Petrograd and other cities east of the war zones. Acute food shortages in the months ahead could be partly explained by the burnt farms and fields the rural people had abandoned. In addition, much of the food that could have been harvested was left to rot because the empire's transportation system, poor to begin with, became almost useless during the war.

Soon, public support for Russia's participation in the hostilities began to crumble. Soon, many representatives to the Duma were publicly criticizing the War Office for its handling of the war.

In the face of growing opposition, Nicholas decided that he himself should become the supreme commander of the troops. He wanted to show his personal devotion to Mother Russia. Some historians ascribe less altruistic motives to Nicholas's behavior. They believe that the czar may have wanted to escape the mounting do-

In September 1915, Nicholas took command of Russia's troops. This photo shows the czar with his generals on the western front in March 1916.

mestic problems of food shortages, a struggling economy, and social unrest.

Nicholas's advisers tried to discourage the czar from implementing this decision. On September 2, 1915, the czar patiently listened to ten of his ministers strongly advise him to reconsider. He responded, "I have heard what you say, but I adhere to my decision."[35]

The Rise of Rasputin

On September 14, 1915, the czar departed from Petrograd and headed for Mogilev—a city safely situated not too near the front—to take command of Russia's troops. When he left, Alexandra was

A 1914 portrait of Nicholas and Alexandra with their four daughters and son Alexis who was afflicted with hemophilia.

The notorious Grigori Efimovich Rasputin—known as the "mad monk"—gained influence over Nicholas and Alexandra after he apparently cured their son's hemophilia.

deeply under the influence of a malign and dangerous man who would soon act as if he alone ruled Russia.

Grigori Efimovich Rasputin was a coarse, crude, scraggly bearded peasant from Siberia whose surname, coincidentally, means "the debauched one." A wandering self-proclaimed man of God, Rasputin was also a prodigious drinker and seducer of women who had earned himself a widespread reputation as a "creature of the devil." Many Russians, rich and poor, had fallen under the so-called holy man's spell. He reportedly had a tremendous level of charisma. One observer said that Rasputin's hypnotic eyes glowed like "two phosphorescent beams of light melting into a great luminous ring."[36]

Part of Rasputin's power lay in the healing powers that were attributed to him. An uncanny ability to heal without the use of medicine became his key to the door of royal power.

Czarina Alexandra had given birth to four daughters; but it was the arrival in

1904 of Alexis, her fifth and last child, that altered Russian history. Alexis, the heir to the throne, was born with hemophilia—the bleeding disease. For those afflicted with this ailment, the tiniest scratch or bruise can cause uncontrollable bleeding and even death.

In November 1905 Alexis suffered a hemorrhage that the royal physicians could not stop. In desperation, the czarina agreed to a suggestion to summon the legendary Rasputin.

The "mad monk" arrived at the Imperial Palace in peasant boots and a caftan. Gently and quietly, Rasputin calmed the boy with prayers and stories, and the bleeding stopped. Overjoyed, Alexandra kissed Rasputin's hand and insisted that her new friend attend the czarevitch whenever necessary. To Alexandra, Rasputin was nothing less than a "miracle" sent by God.

Rasputin was to repeat his successful treatment of the boy many times, and Nicholas and Alexandra became increasingly dependent on his help. In gratitude, they showered Rasputin with favors, enabling him to grow in personal influence and power. In time, he became a friend, adviser, and confidant to the royal couple. Alexandra became so attached to the man she called "Our Friend" that one day enemies of the czar would circulate stories suggesting a romantic involvement.

Gradually, with Alexandra's blessing, Rasputin's power increased until it began to affect the destiny of Russia. Rasputin,

A Vivid Memory

In The Private World of the Last Czar, *Paul and Beatrice Grabbe quote the impression of Meriel Buchanan, daughter of a British ambassador, when she first saw Rasputin.*

"It was a gray, windy day of April in the year 1916 and a heavy fall of snow . . . had made the street almost impassable. . . . An izvoschik [horse-drawn cab], drawn by a shaggy white horse . . . had to stop abruptly just in front of where I was standing. In the izvoschik sat a tall, black-bearded man with a fur cap drawn down over long straggling hair, a bright blue blouse and long high-boots showing under his fur-trimmed overcoat. Pale gray, deep-set but amazingly brilliant eyes were looking at me, and while that gaze held me, I stood motionless . . . held by a sensation of helplessness. . . . Then . . . the driver . . . flicked his horse with his bright green reins and forged on ahead, shouting to the carts to make way for him. With his going a weight of repression lifted from me and I gave a quick sigh of relief, shaking myself as if with that movement I could rid myself of something disturbing and repellent."

for example, named men to fill vacant posts in the Russian Orthodox church. He caused the government officials he did not like to be fired, and made new appointments. Reportedly, Rasputin boasted that he controlled the czarina.

For years, the police dispatched spies to watch Rasputin and keep detailed records of his excessive drinking, fighting, and chasing of women. Prince Yusupov, a nobleman who would later help kill Rasputin, wrote that "His life in Petrograd became a continual revel, the drunken debauch of a galley slave who had come into an unexpected fortune."[37] Alexandra refused to believe such reports, deciding that they were merely mean-spirited attacks on a great religious leader.

In the midst of deprivation, the Russian people, however, were growing ever more resentful of the notorious lecher and the "German woman" (Alexandra) who were running their country. They blamed the two for the widespread famine, poverty, and disorder, and for the disastrous, unpopular war. That Russia was headed for a catastrophe seemed obvious to everyone except Alexandra. Her remedy for Russia's problems? "Be more autocratic, my very own sweetheart," the empress implored in a letter to Nicholas at Mogilev on June 27, 1915.[38]

A month later she complained in another message about "that horrid Rodzyanko" who, as president of the Duma, was calling for a debate concerning the war. "It is not their business . . ." she wrote to her husband, "they must be kept away. . . . Russia, thank God, is not a constitutional country."[39]

Alexandra continued to receive from Rasputin political advice, which she passed on to Nicholas at Mogilev. During this pe-

A cartoon criticizes the liaison between the Romanovs and the lecherous Rasputin. The cartoon depicts Nicholas and Alexandra as Rasputin's puppets.

riod, one of Rasputin's more shocking suggestions was that Alexander Protopopov—a diseased and crazed man who dabbled in the occult—should become minister of the interior.

The empress, a very superstitious person, did not hesitate to make known the monk's choice: "Gregory [Rasputin] earnestly begs you to name Protopopov," she wrote to the czar on September 20, 1916. Two days later she implored him again: "Please take Protopopov as Minister of the Interior. As he is one of the Duma, it will make a great effect and shut their mouths."[40]

Workers protest the naming of the much despised Alexander Protopopov—a diseased and mentally unstable man—as minister of the interior.

Rasputin had his way, and Protopopov was installed on October 3, 1916. This appointment only served to aggravate the worsening situations in Petrograd and on the battlefield. At the same time, food shortages were bringing Russians everywhere to the point of starvation. Strong opposition to the government began to mount in Petrograd. A wave of strikes spread throughout the city, but soldiers sent in to help the police refused to fire on the workers. Although order was finally restored by Cossacks, the emperor's elite mounted troops, czarist authorities were deeply troubled that a military unit had refused to obey a direct command.

Members of the Duma, including conservatives who favored a monarchy, openly denounced both Rasputin and Alexandra. When Nicholas first received reports of these disturbing developments, he began to waver, replacing some government officials with new appointees opposed to Rasputin. Alexandra, horrified by this turnabout, was quick to try to bring her husband back into line. She wrote in December 1916:

> Take no big steps without warning me. . . . Russia loves to feel the whip. . . . How I wish I could pour my will into your veins. . . . I had no sleep, but listen to me, which means Our Friend. . . . Be the emperor . . . crush them all under you. . . . We have been placed by God on the throne, and we must keep it firm and give it over to our son untouched."[41]

At last a small group of powerful Russian nobles decided that Russia could take no more of Rasputin and conspired to murder him. Their motivation, they later claimed, was to save Nicholas, who they perceived as becoming increasingly unpopular because of Rasputin.

One night, as 1916 drew to a close, Rasputin was lured to a party hosted by one of the conspirators—Prince Felix Yusopov. Reportedly Rasputin was plied with food and wine laced with enough poison to kill several men. In a room on a floor above, a small group of conspirators played phonograph recordings and waited anxiously for the poison to take its toll.

But Rasputin only became groggy and angry. Yusopov later recalled that Rasputin

looked at me with a cunning smile. I seemed to hear him say: "You see! You can't do me any harm." But all of a sudden his expression changed into one of fiendish hatred. I felt that he knew why I had brought him there, and what I intended to do to him. A mute and deadly conflict seemed to be taking place between us.[42]

At one point, sounds from the conspirators upstairs caught Rasputin's attention. "What's all that noise?" he asked.

"Probably it's the guests going away," replied Yusopov. "I'll go see."

Yusopov, upset that the murder plan was not working, took that opportunity to leave the room. Minutes later, he returned, holding a pistol behind his back. He offered Rasputin another glass of wine and said, "Grigori Efimovich, you had

A Premonition

Many years after the Russian Revolution, Maria Rasputin, daughter of Russia's most notorious "holy man," recounted in Rasputin, the Man Behind the Myth, *perceptions that are more generous than most. In this passage, she recalls being a terror-stricken child on the night Prince Yusopov came to fetch her father for the fatal evening party.*

"The premonition of danger returned, and no attempt to overcome it could rid me of the feeling that I would never see him [Rasputin] again. I heard the back door close, and heedless of the cold floor, I rushed to the window. It was frosted over, and at first I could not see out. But I rubbed the pane with my fingers until I had made a clear, round area, and there I stood, waiting for my father and the prince to appear.

At last, I heard the crunching footsteps coming from the rear of the house. They came into view, Yusopov holding my father by the arm, as though fearing he would slip away at the last minute. . . .

Feeling helpless and hopeless, I cleared my little patch of clear glass once more and watched as the prince half helped, half pushed my father into the limousine. . . . The automobile left the curb with spinning wheels and sped recklessly down the street. . . .

'Oh, Papa,' I prayed aloud, 'come back to me.' And still weeping, I climbed back into bed, for I had become quite chilled standing at the window and continued to shiver even after I had pulled the covers over me."

better look at the crucifix and say a prayer before it."

Then the prince fired straight at Rasputin's heart. With "a roar as from a wild beast," says Yusopov, Rasputin fell "heavily backwards on the bear-skin rug."[43]

The conspirators huddled over Rasputin. Believing him to be dead, they scattered for a short while to other parts of the palace, discussing the steps that would be needed to cover up their crime.

Minutes later, Yusopov returned to the scene and shook his victim. One of Rasputin's eyes flickered, and the peasant priest lunged at Yusopov, tearing part of the prince's shirt. Rasputin got to his feet and lumbered after the horrified prince up a stairway, through a doorway, and outside into the night.

Just then another conspirator shot Rasputin down. To make sure he was dead this time, Yusopov repeatedly beat the crumpled form with a club. Then the conspirators dumped the corpse into the icy Neva River.

Yusopov claimed that "We . . . [were convinced] . . . that the events of the night would deliver Russia from ruin and dishonour."[44] But the conspirators were wrong. Their deed did virtually nothing to alter the empire's course to destruction.

As Nicholas sped home to comfort his grieving wife, strikes, food riots, antiwar protests, and political turmoil continued to sweep through Petrograd.

The February Revolution

During January 1917, hatred for the czarist regime was so widespread that Russia was swarming with plots to kill or kid-

Demanding freedom from czarist rule, thousands of angry revolutionists storm the streets of Petrograd.

nap Nicholas and Alexandra. But none of them were put into action.

Instead of responding to the growing crisis, Alexandra and Protopopov, the still much despised minister of the interior, busied themselves with séances in an attempt to communicate with Rasputin's spirit. On February 22, 1917, Alexandra wrote Nicholas, who had returned to the front, that

> our dear Friend in the other world also prays for you—He is still so close to us. . . . I think everything will right itself. . . . Only, dearest, be firm, show the power of your fist—that is what the Russians need. You never let a chance pass to show your love and kindness— let them now feel your fist.[45]

Several of the czar's uncles and brothers warned Nicholas that revolution was certain if he failed to act. His curt reply: "I allow no one to give me advice."[46]

On February 23, ominous events began to unfold in Petrograd. Ninety thousand textile workers went on strike during a "Women's Day" commemoration. By the next day, the number of strikers had more than doubled. In the streets, people were shouting, "We want bread! Down with the autocracy! Down with war!"

Students joined the strikers. Mass rallies spontaneously developed throughout the city. Fights erupted with the city police. Streets echoed with gunfire. Streetcars stopped running. Disorder was rampant.

The Petrograd garrison—160,000 soldiers—was sent into the streets to restore order. But, unlike the police, these military troops were reluctant to fire on throngs of people very much like themselves. Their sympathies now were with the masses spoiling for revolution. The troops began to mutiny and join the mobs. Within two days, hardly any of the czar's soldiers who were left were willing to control the swelling masses of Russians.

Greatly alarmed over this development, Duma president Rodzyanko telegraphed an urgent message to the czar at his military headquarters in Mogilev:

> The situation is serious. There is anarchy in the capital. The government is paralyzed. It is necessary immediately to entrust a person who enjoys the confidence of the country with the formation of a government. Any delay is equivalent to death.[47]

The czar fired back a reply: "Stop the disorder in the capital at once."[48]

That order was easier given than obeyed. General Khabalov, the military governor of Petrograd, tried to carry out the czar's commands. Arrests were made. Public meetings were banned. In the end, though, the chaos was beyond his ability to control. Clearly, the power of the czar's government was vanishing forever.

On the streets, some soldiers were firing into crowds. Meanwhile, other uniformed troops continued to mutiny and take up weapons with the rioters.

Soldiers sent to quell uprisings fire rifles in the courtyard of the Winter Palace. Many soldiers, however, were sympathetic to the protesters and joined the mobs.

Defiant Mobs

Both the fearlessness and the determination of the mobs that haunted Petrograd during the February-March wave of revolution can be seen in this excerpt from a police report quoted in Joel Carmichael's Short History of the Russian Revolution.

"In the course of the disorders it was observed . . . that the rioting mobs showed extreme defiance toward the military patrols, at whom, when asked to disperse, they threw stones and lumps of ice dug up from the street. When [warning] shots were fired into the air, the crowd not only did not disperse but answered these volleys with laughter. Only when loaded cartridges were fired into the very midst of the crowd was it found possible to disperse the mob. . . . [Many participants in the mob] . . . however, would . . . hide in the yards of near-by houses, and as soon as the shooting stopped come out again in the streets."

A police report described the fearlessness of the rioting mobs, who showed "extreme defiance toward the military patrols."

Mobs were storming prisons and setting free all inmates—including murderers and thieves. Streets crackled with the sounds of burning buildings. Anarchists ran amok through courtrooms, destroying official files.

The czar's ministers were frantic. The long-feared revolution had arrived. Only this uprising was not the work of the professional revolutionaries; rather, it was the result of a people who had at long last reached a breaking point.

Again Rodzyanko sent the czar a telegram:

> Situation serious. Anarchy in the capital. Government paralyzed. Transport of food and fuel in full disorder. Popular discontent growing. Disorderly firing in the streets. Some military units fire on one another. Essential immediately to order person having the confidence of the country to form new government. Delay impossible. I pray to God that in this hour the blame does not fall on the crown.[49]

Nicholas, upon receiving the telegram, is said to have uttered, "Some more rubbish from that fat Rodyzanko." Then the czar ordered the dissolution of the Duma.

This time, the elected representatives realized the emptiness of the czar's command and refused to disband. After all, soldiers were continuing to mutiny by the thousands and even the police were beginning to defect. Russia's capital city was in chaos. The country was being ripped to shreds by war, famine, and riots. By nightfall on February 27, members of the Duma met at Tauride Palace, wondering if they should be the ones to take charge.

Hours later, in the same building, another group began making plans of its own.

Chapter

5 An Exile's Return

By March 2, 1917, the czar's high-ranking government officials and top generals all agreed that the authority of the czar had collapsed everywhere in Russia. The czar must be told to abdicate (give up the throne) immediately.

On the evening of March 15 in the drawing room of his personal train at the military headquarters in Pskov, Nicholas

In March 1917, Nicholas passed the crown to his brother Mikhail (pictured). Mikhail, however, refused the appointment, bringing three hundred years of Romanov rule to an abrupt end.

received two government representatives who had come to present him with a formal document calling for abdication. The czar took the news quietly. In fact, he seemed tired, and relieved to cast off the burden of running an empire. Without protest, he agreed to step down. By custom, he should have passed the crown to his son. However, the boy was much too young and incurably ill. Thus, Czar Nicholas designated his own brother Mikhail to assume the throne.

Mikhail, however, refused the appointment. And that refusal brought to an abrupt end more than three centuries of Romanov rule in Russia. Autocracy and the days of divine right were over.

The Provisional Government Takes Charge

But who would rule Russia next? The leading contenders were the two hastily created organizations that emerged on the night of February 27 at the Tauride Palace. One was made up of former Duma members who represented the interests of Russia's middle class. The other group called itself the Executive Committee of the Soviet of Workers' and Soldiers'

Deputies, or Ex Com. Its membership consisted of soldiers, workers, Socialist Revolutionaries, and a smattering of Bolsheviks.

Mistrust and hostility between the two groups developed right away. Questions of authority emerged. Which of them had the best claim to rule? Should they share power? Eventually, the members of the Ex Com agreed that the old Duma should lead Russia.

Dismantling the Duma

In this excerpt from The Catastrophe, *quoted in Rhoda Hoff's* Russia: Adventures in Eyewitness History, *Alexander Kerensky, premier of Russia's Provisional Government, tells how Nicholas tried in vain to close down the Duma on March 12, 1917.*

"[At] about eight o'clock in the morning, I was awakened by a voice saying: 'Get up! . . . The Duma has been dissolved, the Volinsk Regiment has mutinied and is leaving its barracks. You are wanted at the Duma at once. . . .'

[Fifteen minutes later] . . . as I approached the Duma, every step seemed to bring me closer to the quivering forces of newly awakened life, and when the aged doorkeeper, as usual, closed the door of the palace behind me, I felt this time as if he were barring behind me forever the way back to the old Russia. . . .

Developments in the city were gathering explosive momentum. One regiment after another had come out into the streets without officers. Some of the officers had been arrested and there were isolated cases of murder. . . . Masses of workmen were pouring into the center of the city. . . . The government machine guns were firing on the people from roofs and belfries. . . .

The council for the party leaders met to consider the situation . . . dominated by one thing only: the realization that Russia was on the brink of ruin. . . .

We . . . demanded that the Duma go immediately into official session, taking no notice whatever of the [czar's] order of dissolution. The majority did not agree with us. The council rejected our proposal. . . .

This refusal to continue in session formally was perhaps the greatest mistake of the Duma. It meant committing suicide at the very moment when its authority was supreme in the country . . . [and] when its strength and influence were at the highest."

Two potential governments emerged in the days following the revolution. One group was made up of former Duma members, and soldiers and workers (pictured) formed the other.

The Ex Com believed that Russia was not yet ready for a socialist revolution. According to Marxist theory, a strong middle-class capitalist society had to develop first, to set the stage for a true socialist revolution. The Provisional Government run by the Duma seemed best able to bring such a class into being.

Many socialists also feared that if the Ex Com seized power and confiscated property too hastily, the upper classes would panic and try to defend themselves by restoring the monarchy.

Authority, however, was about all the Ex Com was willing to yield to the Provisional Government. The new war minister, A.I. Guchko, noted that the Provisional Government possessed no real power.

> Its orders are executed only insofar as this is permitted by the . . . [Ex Com] . . . which holds in its hands the most important elements of actual power, such as troops, railroad, postal and telegraph service. It is possible to say directly that the Provisional Government exists only while this is permitted by the Soviet.[50]

The Ex Com, in fact, also issued its own decrees, such as the well-known Order Number One. Under this command, final authority for the army rested with the Petrograd Soviet, not the Provisional Government. Such an arrangement greatly weakened the Provisional Government and doomed it to failure.

The Provisional Government lost no time in generating a host of reforms. It passed laws granting civil and legal rights for all citizens, banned all forms of discrimination, and declared freedom of speech and press. The death penalty was abolished. The Provisional Government also declared that a nationwide election would be held to choose representatives to a "Constituent Assembly"—a body that would permanently govern Russia.

The early days of the Provisional Government brought jubilant parades and cheering to the streets of Petrograd. Russia, it seemed, was free at last! The decrees from the Provisional Government granted the dreams of generations of Russians.

But were all these reforms enough to quench the revolutionary spirit that still burned in Russia? Most likely the answer is no. True, Rasputin and the Romanovs were gone. But none of the other explosive social, economic, and military problems that had destroyed the czar's government had disappeared. They were only growing worse, and now it was up to the Provisional Government to solve them.

As it happened, however, the Provisional Government made decisions that led straight to failure. For example, it insisted on honoring Russia's commitment to its allies to continue to fight in World War I. As a result, violent antiwar protests erupted across Russia, adding to its wounds and woes.

As for land reform? And food? The Provisional Government believed that these important matters would have to wait until the end of the war. Such a position only served to drive loyal supporters into the arms of the Ex Com.

The Provisional Government also made another costly blunder. It welcomed back all Russians who had been exiled for political reasons during the Romanov years. Many of these former exiles were leaders eager to overthrow the Provisional Government. For Russia's exiled radicals, the fall of the czar meant that the revolution had just begun.

Revolutionary Exiles Return Home

On March 25, 1917, two exiled Russian revolutionaries returned to Petrograd to take control of the Bolshevik's committee: Lev Borisovich Rosenfeld, better known as L.B. Kamenev, and Joseph Vissarionovich Djugashvili. At the time, Kamenev was the more powerful and influential of the two men. But Djugashvili, whose reputation as robber and terrorist

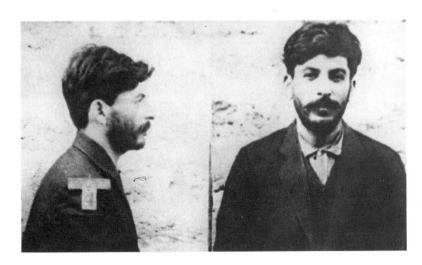

The czar's secret police made these mug shots of the young terrorist Joseph Vissarionovich Djugashvili. This obscure young man came to be known as Joseph Stalin, Russia's most notorious dictator.

for revolutionary causes had caught Lenin's attention, would one day emerge from obscurity to become known worldwide as Joseph Stalin—the most notorious dictator and biggest mass murderer in Russian history.

The Bolsheviks, under the guidance of Kamenev, supported the strategy of waging a defensive war against Germany until revolution in Russia had been completed. Stalin suggested that the Bolsheviks, and their rivals the Mensheviks, reconcile their differences and work together to achieve revolutionary goals.

Lenin's Return

Far away in Switzerland another revolutionary Bolshevik—Vladimir Ilyich Lenin—was unalterably opposed to such ideas. To implement his own vision—that of the Bolsheviks alone taking charge of the revolution—he prepared to join the flood of Russian exiles returning to Russia in the spring of 1917.

On April 9, Lenin and thirty-one other exiled Russians boarded a train in Zurich to take advantage of their new government's offer. A noisy crowd of onlookers had gathered to witness the departure. Some came to cheer, others to jeer.

As the train pulled away at precisely 3:15 P.M., supporters stood along the tracks, waving banners and singing the "Internationale," a song of revolution. Opponents, meanwhile, were hurling words of hate at those on board. "Spies!" they shouted. "German spies!"

Inside the train sat the leader of the group, V.I. Lenin. Serious and somber looking, he had become a short, stocky

Lenin on his way to Petrograd after hearing of the overthrow of the czar.

figure with a domelike head, thin reddish hair, a moustache, and a chin beard.

This was no mere homecoming. Lenin and his fellows were traveling under very mysterious conditions, which would cause controversy for years to come. Authorities in Germany—still Russia's avowed enemy—had arranged the journey, which involved travel through Germany itself and beyond, all the way to Petrograd. The Germans knew that Lenin vehemently opposed Russia's participation in World War I, and they reasoned that if allowed to return to Petrograd, he would try to topple the Provisional Government, which was directing the war effort. Thus, if Lenin ran true to form, and if he succeeded in ousting his enemies, Germany would likewise have one less opponent in the war.

The Germans, however, had one stipulation: the Russian travelers had to remain sealed inside the rail car, to make sure they could not rouse any sort of rebellion as they traveled through Germany. Former British prime minister Winston Churchill coined this grim simile:

> It was with a sense of awe that [the Germans] turned upon Russia the most grisly of all weapons. They transported Lenin in a sealed truck like a plague bacillus from Switzerland to Russia.[51]

Naturally the leaders of the Provisional Government back in Petrograd knew what to expect from Lenin. But they thought the Russian people would eventually turn against him, considering the former exile to be a foreign agent. Thus, the government did nothing to stop Lenin's return.

On April 16, Lenin arrived at Finland Station in Petrograd as cheering crowds of Bolsheviks waved red banners, offering him a hero's welcome. Clearly, many Bolsheviks considered Lenin to be the great driving force of the Revolution, even if he had been in exile. His excited supporters carried him on their shoulders from the platform to the former imperial waiting room inside the station.

Nikolai S. Chkheidze, the Menshevik chairman of the Petrograd Soviet, gave Lenin a cool official welcome, saying he hoped the Bolshevik leader had not come to create "disunion" within the soviet ranks.

Lenin ignored this implied rebuke and forcefully addressed the huge crowd gathered at the station:

> Dear comrades, soldiers, sailors, and workers! I am happy to greet in your persons the victorious Russian Revolution! I greet you as the vanguard of the world proletarian army. . . . Long live the worldwide Socialist revolution![52]

For the remainder of the day, an armored motorcar carried Lenin through the crowded streets. Again and again, from atop the car, he repeated his fiery spiel. Russia must pull out of an imperialist war, which benefited only the ruling

Cheering crowds greet Lenin upon his arrival in Petrograd in April 1917. In return, he pronounced, "I am happy to greet in your persons the victorious Russian Revolution!"

classes in the warring nations! Worldwide revolution of the working classes now!

That night at a Bolshevik gathering, Lenin again unleashed angry criticism. This time he blasted the Executive Committee for its support of the Provisional Government. "We don't need any parliamentary republic," he thundered. "We don't need any bourgeois [middle class] democracy! We don't need any Government except the Soviet of Workers', Soldiers', and Farm-laborers' Deputies."[53]

Furthermore, Lenin insisted, what was needed was another revolution. Armed workers were to become an "iron broom," sweeping away the middle class and all forms of capitalism. Then the workers should seize and operate all banks, farms, and factories.

About a week after his arrival in Petrograd, Lenin restated these views in his *April Theses*, which were published in *Pravda*, the Bolshevik newspaper.

Despite Lenin's objections, the Provisional Government continued to receive cautious support from Ex Com, which was dominated by Mensheviks who had little use for the Bolshevik Lenin. In fact, what Lenin had to say had upset many members of the Soviet. "This is the raving of a madman!" cried one of them. "It's indecent to applaud this claptrap!" Accused another, "Lenin has raised the banner of civil war within the democracy."[54]

At first, Lenin stood almost alone in defense of his radical views. For a while, even other Bolsheviks kept their distance. The editors of *Pravda* wrote that his plan for revolution was "unacceptable."

But Lenin was relentless. He tirelessly argued and harangued to make his points understood. His hard work paid off. Within a month, he managed to get most of his convictions written into official Bolshevik party policy.

Deteriorating conditions in Russia in the spring of 1917 also prompted increasing numbers of people to reconsider Lenin's radical ideas. Popular support of the Provisional Government, in fact, had dropped so much by May that leaders concluded that the only way it could survive at all was to join the Ex Com in a coalition, or partnership, government. Lenin and the Bolsheviks opposed such a merger. "All power to the soviets" was their relentless slogan.

During the middle of June at the First All-Russian Congress of Soviets in Petrograd, Lenin made a bold move. An important Menshevik was publicly denouncing the idea of a forcible takeover of the entire government by the soviets. "There is," the speaker argued, "no political party in Russia which at the present time would say, 'Give us power.'" Lenin interrupted: "There is. . . . Our party will not refuse it. It is ready at any moment to take over the government." Lenin added that given such a chance, his Bolsheviks would arrest fifty to a hundred capitalists and hang them.

At this point, one of the Provisional Government's leading members, a brilliant moderate socialist named Alexander Kerensky, responded, "You Bolsheviks recommend childish prescriptions—arrest, kill, destroy. What are you—socialists or police of the old regime?"[55]

Lenin's words that night foreshadowed things to come. Lenin had clearly outlined his recipe for governing. Under the Bolsheviks there would be no democracy, no elections, and no freedoms. Instead, Lenin and his comrades meant to use the brutish fist of dictatorship.

(Right) Alexander Kerensky (center) became minister of war and kept up the war effort against Germany and Austria. (Bottom) A revolutionary poster reads "The Red Army is the protector of the Proletarian revolution."

By this time, Lenin had won over an important convert to the growing number of Bolsheviks—the former Menshevik Leon Trotsky, who had returned from exile in May. From this point onward, Lenin and Trotsky developed a forbidding and terrifying partnership that forged a revolution.

The July Days

Kerensky became the government's new minister of war, and he too kept up Russia's war effort against Germany and Austria. "Russia could not permit the defeat of her Allies," he said, "for she was linked to them by a common destiny."[56] Like many of his compatriots, Kerensky was also encouraged by the recent entry of the United States into the war, on Russia's side.

But at making war, Kerensky proved no more adept than the czar. What was supposed to be a major offensive on July 1 turned instead into a disastrous retreat for the Russians.

Once more, the Russian people staged angry antiwar protests. By mid-July, angry mobs—often inspired by Bolsheviks—were in the streets, brawling, rioting, and demanding an end to Russia's involvement in World War I. Bands of bullying soldiers prowled the streets, randomly shooting people. Tens of thousands of workers and sailors surrounded the Tauride Palace, threatening to kill government workers inside.

Kerensky was now prime minister. Convinced that these "July days" had gotten out of hand, he ordered the use of military force to crack down on the rioters. The Bolsheviks, who were blamed for inciting the unrest and accused of being "pro-German," were targeted for arrest.

Quite suddenly, Bolshevik leaders were on the run from government forces. Lenin, indicted for treason, fled the country to save himself, this time disappearing into Finland. Trotsky and other Bolshevik leaders, however, were arrested and jailed.

An estimated 2 million people continued to riot in the streets. By late summer, conditions were as bad as they had been during the czar's rule. The major cities faced severe food shortages and constant disorder. Street violence, looting, and arson were commonplace. In the countryside, peasants rampaged, burning country homes and killing members of the upper classes. At the war front, troops were demoralized, underfed, and undersupplied.

A Period of Disintegration

Bruce Lockhart was a young official with the British consular service stationed in Moscow from 1915 to 1917. His well-known book British Agent *provides invaluable insight into the Russian Revolution from the perspective of a high placed foreigner.*

"My own contact with the first revolution [February-March 1917] lasted for eight months. It was a period of depression and disintegration, of a new activity from which all hope and faith had gone. I had been no admirer of the [czar's] regime, but I had little difficulty in realising what the effect of the new [regime] must be on the war [World War I]. Three days after the outbreak of the first rioting I sent off a long [report] of the revolutionary movement to the Embassy. [A summary of the report] . . . in my Diary at the time runs as follows: 'The position is so unclear and so uncertain that any attempt at prophecy is difficult. It seems impossible that the struggle between the bourgeoisie [the middle class] and the proletariat [workers] can be liquidated without further bloodshed. When this will come no one knows, but the outlook for the war is full of foreboding [coming evil].'"

Unwilling to fight for some-body else's interests, Russian soldiers leave the front and make their way home.

Desertions increased. "Peace at any price" became the soldiers' common cry.

That Kerensky was losing power became apparent at a huge political meeting called the Moscow State Congress in August. Some 2,400 delegates representing nearly every political persuasion in Russia (except the Bolsheviks) had gathered to discuss Russia's relentless troubles. Soon, however, liberal and conservative factions began bickering and split into hostile groups. Kerensky could do nothing to bring them together.

Then came a new crisis. Kerensky had appointed General Lavr G. Kornilov as commander in chief of the Russian armies. But when the prime minister began to suspect that Kornilov was planning a military takeover of the government, he abruptly fired the general.

Kornilov refused to give up his post. Instead, he gave orders to his loyal troops to march on Petrograd to take over the government. Clearly, Kerensky was in serious trouble. If Kornilov and the conserva-

tives seized power, all the democratic gains achieved by the Provisional Government might be lost. Worse yet, conservatives might return the former czar from exile and restore the monarchy.

Thus, Kerensky had no choice but to ask for help from the soviets, which included the despised Bolsheviks. The immediate response was overwhelming. Workers armed themselves and formed defense squads to oppose Kornilov's troops. Factories produced ammunition for the workers' brigades. Streets were barricaded. Railway workers diverted trains and kept Kornilov's troops from reaching Petrograd. In the face of such opposition, the general's coup fizzled out on September 16.

Thus, Kerensky's government managed to survive. But for how long? Kerensky was now widely viewed as a weak leader. The Bolsheviks, on the other hand, had grown stronger and more popular as a result of their participation in putting down the threat from Kornilov. Party membership was 200,000, and the Bolsheviks' ragtag military force—the Red Guard—had grown to 25,000 strong.

In late September, the Bolsheviks gained even more power. At a meeting of the Petrograd Soviet, a tumultuous debate took place over the question of leadership. Which faction of socialists should dominate now? A vote was taken, and for the first time ever, the Bolsheviks earned the right to control this all-important soviet. "The new majority applauded like a storm, ecstatically, furiously," recalled Trotsky.[57]

Kerensky could see his power slipping. Because of the Kornilov affair, the army was demoralized and distrusted him. The European allies had grown tired of him.

Kerensky appointed General Kornilov as commander in chief of the Russian armies. Kornilov, in turn, planned a military takeover of the government.

Worst of all, he no longer could count on support from the soviets.

The best course of action seemed to be to work hard toward establishing the goal of the Constituent Assembly—Russia's long dreamed-of permanent government. The first step in this direction was to establish a temporary body called the Preparliament. On October 20, delegates from many political groups met in the Mariinsky Palace in Petrograd. Even the Bolsheviks were there among the 550 representatives. But not for long. At one point, Trotsky stood to denounce the government and

> the propertied classes . . . [who] are openly steering a course for the bony hand of hunger, which is expected to strangle the revolution and the Constituent Assembly first of all. . . . [We] have nothing in common with the murderous intrigue against the people which is being conducted behind the official scenes. We refuse to shield it either directly or indirectly for a single day.[58]

Then amid angry shouts and jeers from the other delegates, Trotsky and sixty fellow Bolsheviks stormed out of the session.

Glad to see them go, most of the other delegates quickly went back to their parliamentary work. However, a few observers realized that the Bolsheviks had done more than simply boycott a political gathering. They had also served notice that from now on they meant to seize power *outside* the framework of government. And they moved swiftly to carry out this goal.

"History will not forgive us," Lenin wrote from his hiding place in Finland, "if

July Days

"Meanwhile the movement was already pouring through the city. The tempest was unleashed. . . . From early evening, lorries and cars began to rush about the city. In them were civilians and soldiers with rifles . . . and . . . frightened-fierce faces. Where they came hurtling from and why—no one knew. . . .

One of the insurgent regiments, led by a Bolshevik lieutenant . . . was an imposing armed force. It was probably enough to hold the city—unless it came up against a similar armed force. The head of the regiment had started to turn . . . when some shots were heard. . . . The commander of the column . . . [riding in a car] . . . turned around and saw the heels of the soldiers, running off in all directions. A few seconds later the car was left alone in the middle of a jeering crowd on the Nevsky Prospect. . . .

The insurgent army didn't know where it should go, or why. It had nothing but a 'mood.' This wasn't enough. The soldiers led by the Bolsheviks, in spite of the complete absence of any real resistance, showed themselves to be really worthless fighting material."

we do not seize power now."[59] However, the Central Committee, which governed the Bolshevik party between party congresses, rejected Lenin's demand and burned his letter.

On October 23, beardless and wearing a red wig on his bald head, Lenin slipped back into Petrograd unnoticed. He made his way to a meeting of the Bolshevik Central Committee, where he insisted that it was time to stage an armed overthrow of the Provisional Government. After much debate, the Central Committee agreed with a resolution stating, "An armed uprising is inevitable and the time is perfectly right!"[60]

Three days later, Trotsky formed the Military Revolutionary Committee (MRC), which would become the military arm of the Bolsheviks. The public was told that Trotsky's group was arming itself to fend off future Kornilov attacks. The truth, of course, was clear to everyone in Petrograd: the Bolsheviks were unmistakably preparing to use force to seize power.

The second Russian Revolution was about to begin.

6 The Second Revolution

The Bolshevik revolution was slated to begin on November 7 (or October 25 according to the Julian calendar, which Russia was still using)—the day the Second All-Russian Congress of Soviets was to meet. The Bolsheviks chose this date deliberately. As historian Michael Kort points out in *The Soviet Colossus*:

> Trotsky reasoned that if the Bolsheviks waited for the Congress to convene and endorse their overthrow of the Provisional Government, the coup would win an important measure of legitimacy. He felt such an endorsement was essential if the Bolsheviks were to avoid strong popular opposition, particularly from the soldiers in Petrograd.[61]

That the Bolsheviks were making ready for an uprising was no secret. Every day Petrograd's newspapers carried stories about what Trotsky's men were planning. The Military Revolutionary Committee headquarters was a beehive of activity and intrigue. Rumors of an upcoming insurgency were sweeping through the city. Cossack troops patrolled the streets, searching for signs of troublemaking.

Red Guards and armored cars patrol Petrograd before the fateful assault on the Winter Palace.

Kerensky was keenly aware of the growing threat. At first, though, he reacted with bluster: "I only wish they would come," he boasted to a British diplomat, "and I will put them down."[62]

But by November 6, the gravity of the impending crisis had registered on Kerensky and his government ministers. That evening, during a cabinet meeting in the Winter Palace, Kerensky declared a state of emergency. Lenin was denounced as a "state criminal." Kerensky issued urgent orders to ban Bolshevik newspapers, arrest Trotsky and his Military Revolutionary Committee [MRC], and put down the activities of the Bolsheviks. The army regiments were to "mobilize on a war footing."

Kerensky's commands, however, failed to accomplish anything much at all. As Trotsky later noted, "it was not indicated who was to carry them out or how."[63]

Until this time, the Bolsheviks lacked a detailed plan of action for an armed takeover of the Provisional Government. Now Kerensky's threat provided them with a purpose: to defend themselves and the Petrograd Soviet against government attack.

As the climax approached, the Bolshevik revolutionaries made last-minute plans in their headquarters at the Smolny Institute, a former school for girls situated along the banks of the Neva River. Meanwhile, for reasons that puzzle many historians, Lenin spent the exciting final hours in a panic, hiding in an apartment in the working section of Vyborg, far from the center of action. Since the Provisional Government had cut telephone lines to the Smolny Institute, he had no way to communicate with the Bolsheviks. Finally, Lenin sent a message to the Bolshevik Central Committee: "With all my power, I wish to persuade the comrades that now everything hangs on a hair. . . . We must at all costs, this evening, tonight, arrest the ministers. . . . We must not wait! We may lose everything."[64]

The Bolsheviks Take Action

Late that evening, armed Bolshevik commandos were ready to move. Every army unit in Petrograd had already been visited by a messenger from Trotsky's MRC. From now on, they were told, take orders from no one but the Bolsheviks.

Around midnight Lenin arrived at Smolny, wearing a wig and a dirty bandage across part of his face to conceal his identity from the Cossacks monitoring activity in the streets. The Bolshevik guards did not recognize him and at first refused him entry. Soon, however, Lenin made his way inside, where Trotsky was going over the final details of the takeover plan. Around 2:00 A.M., Trotsky looked at his watch and said, "It's begun."

Trotsky's men went into action. MRC units fanned out across Petrograd and occupied the post office, the central telegraph office, important bridges, railway stations, the State Bank, a main electric power station, and several important government buildings. And they met with no real resistance.

Later that morning many Petrograd residents awoke, ate breakfast, and went to work quite unaware of the extraordinary events taking place around them. Street cars ran on schedule. Shops opened for business. The opera house staged a performance. For the most part, the Bolshevik revolution was being carried out efficiently, quietly, and almost bloodlessly.

At ten o'clock that morning, Lenin issued a statement that the Provisional Government had fallen from power and the Military Revolutionary Committee was in charge of Russia. Although such a proclamation was premature, some 20,000 Red Guards were at the moment prowling the streets of Petrograd, taking over one city block after another. By the end of the day, the Bolsheviks controlled the whole city except the Winter Palace, which was the headquarters of Kerensky's government. "From being on the run to supreme power—that's too much," Lenin observed. "It makes me dizzy."[65]

At dusk, Red Guard troops and armored cars began surrounding the Winter Palace. Kerensky was not there, however. Earlier that day he had fled Petrograd in a car bearing an American flag. He had gone to the city of Gatchina 28 miles away, with the hope of rallying the Third Cavalry Corps to put down the Bolshevik uprising.

Around seven o'clock that evening, two members of the Red Guard pedaled bicycles up to the Winter Palace and hand delivered an ultimatum to the thirteen members of the Provisional Government inside: surrender to the Bolsheviks within twenty minutes, or face an armed attack.

The ministers refused to give in. Standing by to protect them and a few hundred members of the Provisional Government were 300 Cossack troops, 1,000 military cadets, and 130 members of an all-woman "Amazon" brigade.

For the next two hours, sporadic small-arms and cannon fire could be heard in the area, but nothing resembling all-out

An all-woman "Amazon" brigade guards the Winter Palace in an attempt to protect the Provisional Government headquartered there.

During the assault on the Winter Palace, Bolshevik-led soldiers, sailors, and Red Guards occupied key locations in Petrograd. Here, bayonet-armed seamen from the cruiser Aurora *stand ready for action.*

combat had taken place. At 9:40 P.M. sailors on board the cruiser *Aurora*, which had just come up the Neva River, saw a purplish signal flare go up from the nearby Peter and Paul fortress. This was the sign they had been waiting for. Immediately, ship's cannon opened fire with blanks to announce a general attack.

On cue, the Red Guard began attacking the palace more enthusiastically. Rifle shots and the chattering of machine guns echoed in the night. But little resistance came from inside the Winter Palace.

An hour later, the ministers of the Provisional Government were aghast when the 300 Cossacks loaded their equipment onto their horses and left the palace area. They were, they said, finished fighting. Clearly, support for the government was melting away.

About this time, members of the Duma located elsewhere in the city had learned about the assault on the Winter Palace. They decided to march to the palace to "die together with the government." They

didn't get far. Bolshevik sailors stopped them from entering the combat area.

In future years, communist propagandists would use print and film to dramatize in grand heroic terms the storming of the Winter Palace. Many historians, however, prefer to describe much of what happened that night as a comedy of errors. In addition, despite the gunfire, there is ample evidence that both sides tried to avoid bloodshed. The Bolshevik uprising cost fewer than twenty casualties.

The Winter Palace occupied four-and-a-half acres and had so many entrances and corridors that no one could keep track of exactly who was going where. Some palace military cadets and the entire women's brigade, for example, were caught by Red Guards as they tried to slip out of the palace.

On the other hand, for a while, Red Guards kept entering the palace only to be arrested and disarmed by the cadets. The situation became so confusing that at one point a defending officer cried out, "How

Property of the People

The American jour-nalist John Reed wit-nessed firsthand the storming of the Winter Palace in St. Peters-burg. Here is an ex-cerpt from his classic work, Ten Days That Shook the World.

"Here [along the way to the Winter Palace] it was abso-lutely dark, and nothing moved but pickets of soldiers and Red Guards grimly intent. . . . Soldiers were stand-ing in every doorway talking in low tones. . . . At the cor-ners patrols stopped all passersby. . . . The shooting had ceased. . . .

Carried along by the eager wave of men we were swept into the right-hand entrance, opening into a great bare vaulted room, the cellar of the East wing, from which issued a maze of corridors and staircases. A num-ber of huge packing cases stood about, and upon these the Red Guards and soldiers fell furiously, battering them open with the butts of their rifles, and pulling out carpets, curtains, linens, porcelain plates, glassware. . . . One man went strutting around with a bronze clock perched on his shoulder; another found a plume of os-trich feathers, which he stuck in his hat. The looting was just beginning when somebody cried, 'Comrades! Don't touch anything! Don't take anything! This is the prop-erty of the People!' Many hands dragged the spoilers down. Damask and tapestry were snatched from the arms of those who had them; two men took away the bronze clock. Roughly and hastily the things were crammed back in their cases, and self-appointed sen-tinels stood guard. . . . Through corridors and up stair-cases, the cry could be heard growing fainter and fainter in the distance, 'Revolutionary discipline! Property of the People.'"

many are already in the Palace? And who, in fact, occupies the Palace? We or the Bol-sheviks?"[66]

Around eleven o'clock that night, the Bolsheviks inside the palace were numer-ous enough to begin disarming the cadets. Soon, the gunfire and excitement petered out. At 1:50 A.M., the thirteen government ministers sat businesslike at a table, as Bol-sheviks entered the meeting room and surrounded them.

"This is the Provisional Government," greeted one of the ministers. "What is your pleasure?"

Vladimir A. Antonov-Ovseyenko, who was in charge of the Bolshevik guard, haughtily replied, "I announce that all of you members of the Provisional Government are under arrest. . . . Hail the proletariat and its Revolutionary Soviets."[67]

The Bolsheviks Grab National Power

All night, during the storming of the Winter Palace, a rowdy smoke-filled session of the All-Russian Congress of Soviets had been under way at Smolny. Mensheviks, Bolsheviks, and Socialist Revolutionaries were all engaged in a frenzied debate as the night wore on. This time, though, the Bolsheviks were in the majority of delegates.

The Mensheviks and other socialist groups were furious over the Bolsheviks' ongoing use of force. At one point a delegate moved that the Congress negotiate with the Provisional Government, but Trotsky shouted, "No compromise is possible. To those who tell us to do this we must say: you are miserable bankrupts, your role is played out. Go where you ought to be: into the dustbin [garbage can] of history."[68]

Eventually, many Mensheviks and SRs did storm out of the meeting. Finally, at about 2:30 A.M., the chairman interrupted the proceedings to read an important announcement that confirmed the inevitable: the ministers who had been gov-

Bolshevik forces storming the Winter Palace are heroically portrayed in a Soviet painting. Although much communist propaganda dramatizes the assault in grand terms, many historians have described the event as a comedy of errors.

erning from the Winter Palace were under arrest. The Provisional Government had ceased to exist.

And a new regime had just arrived. Later that evening, its undisputed leader took the podium during another session of the Congress of Soviets. John Reed, a young American journalist sympathetic to the Bolsheviks, recalls Lenin's appearance:

A short, stocky figure, with a big head set down in his shoulders, bald and bulging. Little eyes, a snubbish nose, wide, generous mouth and heavy chin . . . clean shaven now, but already beginning to bristle with the well-known beard of his past and future. Dressed in shabby clothes, his trousers were much too long for him. Unimpressive, to be the idol of a mob, loved and revered as perhaps few leaders in history have been.[69]

Lenin pronounced to a cheering crowd, "We shall now proceed to construct the Socialist order!"[70] That same night a committee composed entirely of Bolsheviks was set up to run the country.

But a slew of problems greeted the self-appointed government. Opposition to the Bolsheviks quickly arose. The next day, in fact, Kerensky was leading a military force back to Petrograd to battle the Bolsheviks. In the meantime, bloody fighting was under way in Moscow between forces loyal to the Provisional Government and those who backed the Bolsheviks. Within a few days, however, Kerensky's effort failed and the Bolsheviks defeated their enemies in Moscow. The Bolshevik victory was total.

Revolutionary Changes

To the casual observer in Petrograd, nothing seemed different immediately after the Bolsheviks seized power. But soon radical changes in Russian life were under

Long Live the Revolution

According to Michael Morgan's Lenin, *at 10 A.M. on October 25, 1917, as the Bolsheviks were completing their takeover of Petrograd, Lenin released this proclamation:*

"The Provisional Government has been deposed. State power had passed into the hands of the . . . [Bolsheviks]. . . .

The cause for which the people have fought, namely, the immediate offer of a democratic peace, the abolition of landed proprietorship, workers' control over production, and the establishment of Soviet power—this cause has been secured.

Long live the revolution of workers, soldiers, and peasants."

way. Hundreds of government decrees were issued by the Bolsheviks. Farmland was to be confiscated from landlords and divided among the peasants. Peace talks with Germany were called for. Nobles were to lose their titles. There was to be a clear separation of church and state. Women were to be given rights equal to those of men. Teaching religion in the schools was banned.

Marx had predicted that when a successful proletarian revolution took place, a workers' "dictatorship" would emerge and rule the country. Thus, argued Lenin, at this moment in the Bolshevik revolution, the Bolsheviks themselves would provide that dictatorship . . . on behalf of the workers. This meant that the Bolsheviks were free to do whatever they pleased and claim they were being true to Marxist principles.

First, however, the Bolsheviks had to face up to a pressing problem: a national election for the Constituent Assembly was scheduled for November 25. The idea of representative government was still immensely popular in Russia. The Bolsheviks, in fact, had publicly favored the idea. To cancel the election would invite a firestorm of protest and awaken distrust across the land. Thus, the Bolsheviks had little choice but to go ahead with the scheduled vote.

It was a decision they soon regretted. When all the 41.6 million votes were tallied, it was clear that the Socialist Revolutionaries had won the majority of delegates. The Bolsheviks, who carried 175 seats out of 707, or about 25 percent of the vote, had lost their legal authority to rule.

Lenin and his cohorts, however, were not about to walk away from power. When the first duly elected Constituent Assembly met on January 18, 1918, armed Bolsheviks shut it down at gunpoint.

The next day, the doors to the Constituent Assembly were locked; democracy in Russia was dead, strangled in its infancy by the very people who had once promised personal freedoms. The Bolsheviks, in fact, had betrayed many of their promises during their brutal struggle to become the most powerful force in Russia.

"The War is Relentless"

Lenin would keep his promise to end the war, however. "The War is relentless," he had written. "It puts the alternative in a ruthless relief, either to perish, or to catch up with the advanced countries and outdistance them, too, in economic matters."[71]

Negotiations were begun with Germany. Russia's representatives, led by Trotsky, were initially shocked by Germany's severe demands for peace. Trotsky resorted to stalling tactics, hoping that German workers would follow the Bolshevik example and launch their own socialist revolution.

German workers, however, did not revolt, and when German military forces began to march deeper into Russia, the Bolsheviks came to terms at the negotiating table.

On March 3, 1918, Lenin signed the Treaty of Brest-Litovsk that ended Russia's involvement in World War I. Russia had peace; but the cost was catastrophic. With a stroke of Lenin's pen, Russia had given Germany one-third of its farmlands and populations, four-fifths of its coal mines, one-fourth of its railways and one-third of its factories. Even worse, the victors exacted that war reparations be made.

Russians were shocked and angered when they learned the steep price of peace. Lenin, though, was unmoved by their protests. A communist revolution would eventually spread to Germany, he argued, and maybe even worldwide, just as Karl Marx had predicted; by then the treaty would not be enforceable.

Lenin had also hoped that the peace with Germany would give Russia a chance to concentrate on economic reform. "Let us give away space," he said, "but gain time."[72]

There was no extra time. Instead, the shattered empire was soon to undergo yet another wave of mass killing. In the wake of Russia's humiliating withdrawal from World War I, Poland and Finland decided to revolt against Russia. Moreover, widespread resistance to the Bolsheviks was developing among the ethnic Russians. Workers began to strike again in the cities. Infuriated Socialist Revolutionaries launched a renewed campaign of terrorism and assassination, this time against Bolsheviks. John Reed writes:

> All were against [the Bolsheviks]—businessmen, speculators, investors, landowners, army officers, politicians, teachers, students, professional men, shopkeepers, clerks, agents. The other socialist parties hated the Bolsheviks with an implacable hatred.[73]

In response, the Bolsheviks unleashed the Cheka, or "Extraordinary Commission," a ruthless secret police force, authorized to destroy all opposition. Books, magazines, and newspapers unfavorable to the Bolsheviks were censored. Opponents were killed, making a mockery of the abolition of the death penalty. Terror was unleashed on the country to force unquestioning obedience. "Do you think we can be victors without the most severe revolutionary terror?" Lenin asked his followers.[74] So murderous and so brutal was the Cheka that in the years to come the sum

A treaty signed at Brest-Litovsk in March 1918 ended Russia's involvement in World War I. The price of peace, however, was steep: Russians were forced to give away abundant land and property and make war reparations.

Bolshevik Violence

In Ten Days That Shook the World, *John Reed provides an example of the resistance to the Bolsheviks' violent takeover by quoting from this pamphlet distributed in Petrograd in November 1917.*

"To the Attention of All Citizens.
The State Bank Is Closed!
Why?
Because the violence [caused by the Bolsheviks] . . . against the State Bank has made it impossible for us to work. The first act of the People's Commissars [the Bolshevik leadership] was to DEMAND TEN MILLION RUBLES, and on November 27th THEY DEMANDED TWENTY-FIVE MILLIONS, without any indication as to where this money was to go.

. . . We functionaries [bank workers] cannot take part in plundering the people's property. We stopped work.

CITIZENS! The money in the State Bank is yours, the people's money, acquired by your labour, your sweat and blood. CITIZENS! Save the people's property from robbery, and us from violence, and we shall immediately resume work.

EMPLOYEES OF THE STATE BANK."

of its atrocities would far exceed those committed by the forces of the Romanovs.

Perhaps the Bolsheviks controlled Petrograd, Moscow, and most of central Russia, but in the southern part of Russia, anti-Bolshevik governments were developing. Here and there guerrilla bands and small armies of men were vowing to carry on the war against Germany, despite the treaty. They were prepared to fight the Bolsheviks too. Eventually, these groups—former czarists, plus socialists, SRs, democrats, and a hodgepodge of others—would gather into a massive single effort to destroy the Bolsheviks. They called themselves the "Whites" to distinguish themselves from the Bolsheviks, with their red flag and Red Guards.

The Bolsheviks in this period began to call themselves Communists, and the All-Russia Communist party was formed in 1918. Russia was headed for civil war.

7 Russia at War with Itself

The Russian civil war was prompted by an unexpected event in April 1918. After Russia officially quit the battlefield, a huge number of enemy troops remained stranded in Russia. Called the Czech Legion, this military force was made up of 30,000 Czechoslovakian draftees and deserters from the Austrian army. Few of these troops, however, were eager to keep on fighting with the Germans and Austrians. Instead, the legion decided to switch sides and fight with Russia's former allies—England and France. Czech nationalists were at this time trying to create an independent state free of Austrian rule, and the soldiers thought that they could gain support for their efforts by giving their allegiance to France and England.

A decision was made to transport the Czechs by train on the Trans-Siberian Railway to Vladivostok, on Russia's Pacific coast. From here, the soldiers were to be transported by ship to the United States, and then to western Europe to fight with the French against Germany and Austria.

The long troop trains were already under way, however, when Communist officials in Petrograd decided a different route should be used. They dispatched new orders: the trains were to be diverted

The Bolsheviks' political situation was complicated by a rising wave of anti-Communist dissent. When civil war broke out, the Whites, pictured here at Vladivostok, set out to rout the communist regime.

A battle site during Russia's civil war. Early on, the tide of battle appeared to favor the Whites. Trotsky, in turn, welded the Red Army into a powerful fighting force.

to the cities of Archangel and Murmansk, both located on Russia's north Atlantic coast. This switch in plans meant that the locomotives had to retrace some of the distance already covered, to make connections with a different set of tracks. The Czechs on board became suspicious but did not desert the train.

During a stopover in the Siberian town of Chelyabinsk, Czech soldiers encountered Austrian and Hungarian prisoners of war who angrily denounced the Czechs as traitors. A fight developed which led to the lynching of a Hungarian soldier and a riot.

In Moscow, alarmed Communist officials ordered the Czechs to surrender their weapons. The legion refused to comply. Trotsky was furious; he telegraphed another message: the Czechs were not only to be forced to disarm, their units were to broken up and the troops forced to join the Russian Red Guards and groups of laborers. Trotsky also ordered a stop to all eastward movement of the troop trains.

The Czechs were angered by this command. All along vast stretches of railway, they took over towns and rail stations and set up encampments, prepared to fight the Communists at all cost. Their defiance proved to be just the inspiration many Russian anti-Communist groups were waiting for. Soon, across central Russia and elsewhere the Czechs were joined by the anti-Communist Whites. Soon, the Whites began attacking from all directions. Their targets included the cities of Moscow (the Communists' new capital), Petrograd, Archangel, Vladivostok, and Murmansk.

The old empire was dissolving. Finland and Poland bolted from Russian control and formed independent governments. The Baltic lands also broke away and formed the new nations of Estonia, Latvia, and Lithuania. Separatist rumblings came from the Ukraine and Siberia.

Disturbed by this new disorder, Russia's former allies—Britain, France, and the United States—sent military troops to Vladivostok, Archangel, and Murmansk to prevent leftover Allied war materiel from falling into Communist hands. The Allies opposed the rise of Communist power because they feared that nationalization of Russian industries, which the Bolsheviks had supported, would result in the loss of their investments in Russia. The Allies were also concerned about the continuous Bolshevik call for a worldwide workers' revolution.

Trotsky's Rise to Military Leadership

Although he had been an amateur in military affairs, Leon Trotsky—now a fox-faced man with a goatee and a moustache—had proven his mettle as the cre-

ator and leader of the revolutionary MRC. But could he command a military force vast and disciplined enough to subdue an entire nation in rebellion?

When the worker-militia of the Red Guards proved weak in battle against the Whites, Trotsky realized he had to use drastic measures to create a more powerful fighting force. One of his first steps was to draft 5 million civilians into the Red Army. He also recruited more than 48,000 experienced czarist officers. To guarantee their cooperation, Trotsky threatened to kill them and harm their families.

Once the troops were in place, Trotsky rushed across Russia in an armored train, traveling from one battle site to another, gathering information, giving orders, and

Red Army troops parade in Kharkov during the final year of the war. Their superior fighting ultimately crushed anti-Communist forces in the civil war.

Gathering Information

Among the many tasks facing a military leader is the gathering of accurate information on which to base battlefield decisions. In Lenin, *Michael C. Morgan quotes Trotsky on this subject.*

"After making the round of a division and [figuring out] its needs on the spot I would hold a conference in the staff car or the dining-car, inviting as many representatives as possible, including those from the lower commanding grades and from the ranks as well as from the local Party organization, the Soviet administration, and the trade unions. In this way I got a picture of the situation that was neither false nor high-coloured. These conferences always had practical results."

Trotsky in Moscow in 1919. During the turbulent years of the war, Trotsky proved himself a formidable military leader.

encouraging, inspiring, and exhorting the Red Army to achieve victory. His work paid off. The Red Army became a formidable fighting force.

The Communists used questionable methods to wipe out remaining civilian dissent during the civil war years (1918-1921). The Cheka extended its mission to destroy all "enemies of the people" be-

yond Petrograd and Moscow to the rest of Russia. Soviet headquarters everywhere received Cheka orders to "seek out, arrest, and shoot immediately" all those opposed to the Communist revolution. The results of the Cheka's efforts, now referred to as the Red Terror, were horrendous. As many as 50,000 people were killed by this dreaded organization in 1918 alone.

Czar Nicholas and his family in exile before their violent execution on July 16, 1918.

The Czar's End

When civil war broke out, the former czar and his family were living a gloomy existence under house arrest in Ekaterinburg (present-day Sverdlovsk), a town in the foothills of the Ural Mountains. For some time, Lenin and members of his inner circle had considered staging a public trial in which Nicholas would be accused of a variety of crimes. Trotsky had visions of himself as chief prosecutor.

But by July 12, 1918, Czech forces were rapidly approaching Ekaterinburg. There was no longer time to mount a trial. The Communists realized that the czar might be freed, to become a living symbol for diehard conservatives and monarchists. "Ilyich [Lenin] believed we shouldn't leave the Whites a live banner to rally around," wrote Trotsky years afterward.[75]

Though it is not clear which, if any, high official in Moscow approved the idea, the local soviet in Ekaterinburg met on the night of July 14 and reached a grim decision expressed in a top-secret edict. "The meeting unanimously agreed to liquidate the former Czar Nikolai Romanov and his family and also those in his service . . . and the responsibility for this was given to Comrade Yurovsky, Ya.— member of the Cheka."[76]

On the night of July 16, the czar and his family were abruptly awakened by Communist guards. They were told that because trouble was brewing nearby, they all must be evacuated to safety by automobile. The Romanov family quickly got out of bed and dressed. Then Nicholas and Alexandra, their two daughters and son, their pet dog, three personal servants, and a family doctor all followed Yurovsky, the Cheka commando, who led them by kerosene light to a semibasement room. The czar carried his ailing boy.

Chairs were provided for the czar and his wife and son. From outside came the sound of a car engine starting. Just then Yurovsky and eleven other Cheka commandos entered the room.

Yurovsky quickly got to the point: "Nikolai Alexandrovich, by the decision of the Urals District Committee we are going to shoot you and your family."[77]

"What?" gasped Nicholas, holding onto thirteen-year-old Alexis.

Yurovsky promptly responded by using his revolver to shoot the czar in the head. Immediately, the other commandos opened fire on the czar's family and entourage. The Romanovs' daughters screamed amid a hail of bullets. One of the girls survived briefly and was bayoneted to death. Minutes later, all the bloodied victims were dead. The little dog too lay motionless beside the slain. Trotsky wrote that

the execution of the Tsar's family was needed, not only to frighten, horrify, and dishearten the enemy, but also to shake up our own ranks to show them that there was no turning back, that ahead lay either complete victory or complete ruin.[78]

Attack on Lenin

Lenin himself became a victim of this climate of violence. In August the revolutionary leader was attending a meeting at an industrial plant in a suburb of Moscow. As he was leaving the building, a young black-haired woman named Fanny Kaplan came alongside, engaging him in conversation. As Lenin began to enter his chauffeur-driven car, Kaplan suddenly produced a pistol. "Traitor!" she exclaimed and fired five times. Four bullets entered Lenin's body. As he crumpled onto the pavement, Kaplan sprinted away but was soon caught.

During Lenin's painful convalescence, the Cheka questioned the young woman until she told all. Kaplan revealed that she

The Red Terror

According to Richard V. Allen, Hall Bartlett, and Kenneth Colegrove in Democracy and Communism, Theory and Action, *a secret police agent explained the Cheka's mindset this way:*

"We are no longer waging war on individuals, we are exterminating the bourgeois [members of the middle class] as a class. Do not look into the record of the accused for proof as to whether or not he opposed the Soviet government by word or deed. The first question that should be asked is this: To what class does he belong and of what extraction, what education and what profession? These questions should decide the fate of the accused. This is the meaning and purpose of the Red Terror."

The civil war came to a close in the fall of 1920, yet left behind a horrifying trail of death and destruction.

was a Socialist Revolutionary who had been sentenced to eleven years in prison for trying to kill a czarist official. Freed during the great amnesty of political prisoners declared by the Provisional Government in 1917, she later targeted Lenin for assassination because, she said, he had betrayed the Revolution.

According to some accounts, when the Cheka had no more use for Kaplan, they shot her dead. One-time Bolshevik Angelica Balabanoff, however, later claimed that because Lenin had expressed qualms over executing a revolutionary comrade, Kaplan was exiled to Siberia, not executed.

Whatever Kaplan's fate may have been, the Communists wanted to extract an even greater punishment from their enemies for the attempt on Lenin's life. In retribution, they rounded up 500 suspected opponents: "those living under assumed names . . . everyone mixed up with White Guards . . . and other dirty plotters against the government"[79] and executed them.

The Civil War Ends

The horror, brutality, and inhumanity of the civil war had devastating effects on people everywhere in the crumbling empire. As historian Michael Kort wrote, all sides committed unspeakable atrocities:

> Both Red and White forces spread their terror across the land in a desperate struggle—and they did not have the field to themselves. Bands of peasant guerrillas known as "Greens," driven by motives ranging from anarchist ideals to pure banditry, fought

both the Reds and the Whites and ravaged both the countryside and towns.[80]

By the spring of 1920, the Red Army had triumphed over most of the White forces. Wherever cities were recaptured from the Whites in battle, the Cheka followed up with the Red Terror and took the lives of thousands of civilians.

In April the civil war was approaching its conclusion; the Red Army was chasing a retreating Polish army all the way back to Poland. Lenin believed that a conquered Poland offered an opportunity to spread the workers' revolution into western Europe. The Poles, however, stopped the Reds just outside the gates of Warsaw.

A decisive Red victory in the Crimea in the south of Russia brought the Russian civil war to an end during the autumn of 1920.

Communist Rule

Many factors figured in the Communist victory. Clearly, Trotsky's military expertise had played a major role. The Red Army's peasant soldiers also made a decisive difference. These men were willing to do anything to keep the hated nobles from returning to power, whereas weariness of war and lack of unity had helped to defeat the Whites. At one point, for example, there were eighteen different White governments. Finally, with the conclusion of World War I in 1918, the Allies saw little reason to remain in Russia and departed, leaving the Whites to confront the Reds alone.

The victorious Communist forces now faced a nation in economic, social, and political shambles, and their plans for renewal only made things worse. During the years 1918 to 1921 in accordance with a policy designated "War Communism," the Communists tried to forcibly impose Marxist ideas on the Russian economy. Private property was abolished. Russia's major industries were nationalized. Every able-bodied worker between the ages of sixteen and fifty was forced to work on behalf of the government. In the countryside, peasants were made to toil on "collective" state farms. They also had to turn over to the government food grown on their own farms. Food so appropriated was destined for the Red Army. Sometimes the farmers were not paid at all; at other times they received payment at rates set artificially low. When famine loomed, Lenin urged gangs of workers and peasants to go to the

A starving child during the Russian famine in 1921. After its civil war, Russia was devastated by famine, despair, and social breakdown.

The remnants of the railroad station at the Kronstadt naval base, where the Red Army suppressed a revolt on March 17, 1921.

countryside to steal food, particularly from the wealthier peasants, or kulaks. As a result, many peasants merely stopped producing. Some even burned their crops to keep them from being confiscated by the government. By 1921, farms were producing only half of what they had in 1913.

Everywhere there was unemployment, famine, despair, and social breakdown. Inflation had destroyed the value of the Russian ruble. Millions were homeless. War orphans rooted for food among burned-out homes. Cannibalism was rumored to have occurred in the countryside. A typhus epidemic, which began in 1913, killed so many people that during winter bodies had to be stacked at the cemeteries until spring came and thawed the earth. A total of 7 million people may have died from hunger and disease as a result of the disruption of the civil war.

Still more horror came in 1921 when a drought brought famine and death to another 5 million people. Much to Lenin's annoyance, the Communists had no choice but to accept help from the United States, Britain, and France, which sent in grain and relief supplies to stave off death on an even more massive scale.

By the early 1920s, writes historian Isaac Deutscher, Soviet Russia

> stood alone, bled white, starving, shivering with cold, consumed by disease, and overcome with gloom. In the stench of blood and death her people scrambled wildly for a breath of air, a faint gleam of light, a crust of bread. "Is this," they asked, "the realm of freedom? Is this where the great leap has taken us?"[81]

In February 1921 many Russians had had enough of communism. New revolts began taking place. In Petrograd, factory workers went on strike. The next month some 25,000 sailors at the Kronstadt naval base also struck in support of the workers. These sailors had helped the Bolsheviks come to power. And what the sailors wanted now was what they always had wanted: freedom and democracy, not dictatorship.

In the end, the Kronstadt sailors paid a dear price for their bold actions. Trotsky dispatched the Red Army to the Kronstadt fortress. Here, on March 17, reluctant soldiers opened fire on their rebelling military comrades, killing thousands.

Partial Return to Free Enterprise

Faced with such deteriorating conditions, Lenin was forced to take an action that infuriated other Bolsheviks: in the autumn of 1921 he allowed Russians a partial return to free enterprise. Lenin's new plan, called the New Economic Policy (NEP) was a compromise between the free enterprise system and communism. Small businesses and factories were returned to their owners. Russia's major factories, however, remained nationalized. Food growers could now farm their own land. And their products would be taxed, not confiscated. Once more, workers received money wages instead of food and clothing. During these reforms, many hard-line Communists criticized Lenin for betraying his Marxist ideals. Nevertheless, the NEP provided a period of relative prosperity. Pure communism, Lenin asserted, could come later.

Although the Reds had masterminded a revolution and brutally put down a murderous civil war, the average Russian who had once placed so much hope in the Revolution, must have grieved over what Russia had become. A disillusioned radical, the novelist-playwright-critic Maxim Gorky, wrote:

Everything I said about the savage Bolsheviks is true, about their cruelty which approaches sadism, about their lack of culture, about their ignorance of the psychology of the Russian peo-

A Legacy of Death and Destruction

The British writer H.G. Wells visited Leningrad in 1920 and included this firsthand account of Russian misery caused by continuous war and revolution in his book The Outline of History.

"[Leningrad was] . . . an astonishing spectacle of desolation. . . . Nothing had been repaired for four years. There were great holes in the streets where the surface had fallen into the broken drains; lamp-posts lay as they had fallen; not a shop was open, and most were boarded up over their broken windows. The scanty drift of people in the streets wore shabby and incongruous clothing, for there were no new clothes in Russia, no new boots. Many people wore bast [fiber] wrapping on their feet. People, city, everything were shabby and threadbare. Even the Bolshevik commissars had scrubby chins, for razors and such-like things were neither being made nor imported. The death-rate was enormous, and the population of this doomed city was falling by the hundred thousand every year."

Russian peasants prepare to harvest their crops on land that Lenin decreed was their own in 1921.

ple, about the fact that they are performing a disgusting experiment on the people and are destroying the working class—all this and much more that I said about "Bolshevism" retains its full force.[82]

Russia was renamed in July 1918 as The Russia Soviet Federated Socialist Republic (RSFSR). The Constitution, which was the legal basis for this new nation, called for elections and "a free union of the peoples of Russia." But Lenin had no intention of allowing such freedom. The Communist party ruled as a dictatorship and the Red Army made sure no non-Russian group could break away from the RSFSR. By 1922, the Communists had a new name for their country, The Union of Soviet Socialist Republics.

In May 1922 Russia was rocked by a new turn of events. Lenin suffered from the first of several serious strokes. He became an invalid. His right hand and leg were paralyzed. His speech was slurred. His end was coming.

As Lenin neared death, Russia was about to enter what some historians later called the third, or "return to stability," stage of the Revolution. Compared with the French Revolution, Russia now awaited its Napoleon.

Who would that be?

Chapter

8 Perverting the Goals of the Revolution

When Lenin died on January 22, 1924, at the age of fifty-three, Russia grieved. To millions of former Bolsheviks the leader of the Russian Revolution was not just a great leader and a hero, but a near-god. How, they wondered, could the Revolution continue without him?

However, millions of others—former Whites and others who despised the Communist dictatorship—rejoiced. They had hated Lenin and would never forget the terror and horror inflicted by his brutal regime.

Although Lenin's widow had asked that the funeral be kept simple, the event turned into an elaborate public affair. The corpse was preserved and dressed in a khaki military-style jacket, and the red coffin was equipped with a glass lid to permit public viewing. For decades to come, Russians and visitors to Moscow from around the world would parade past the mausoleum on Red Square to glimpse Lenin's embalmed corpse. An almost religious devotion to the memory of Lenin developed. In keeping with an old Russian tradition of preserving and venerating the bones of saints and czars, many Russians in effect turned Lenin's mausoleum into a shrine.

With Lenin gone, the Revolution was at a crossroads. The Communist party degenerated, and there was bitter fighting

An ailing Lenin appears with family members in a photo taken in 1922. He died two years later at the age of fifty-three.

over who should succeed Lenin. The leading contenders were nicknamed the Professor and the Peasant.

Trotsky—the so-called professor—had been Lenin's comrade and right-hand man. A scholar and intellectual, orator, journalist, military genius, Trotsky was one of the Revolution's most brilliant stars.

Trotsky's chief rival was a pock-faced man with a burly dark moustache, a withered arm, and webbed toes. He was Joseph V. Djugashvili, better known as Stalin—man of steel—who served as the general secretary of the Communist party.

Stalin came from Georgia, a formerly autonomous region of Russia where revenge and blood feuds were common. As a peasant youth, he had studied for the priesthood in the Russian Orthodox church, until he was expelled. Later, as a revolutionary, Stalin robbed banks to raise money for radical groups and spent much

Stalin (right) sits with Lenin in a photo taken near the time of Lenin's death. Before he died, Lenin warned that he did not want Stalin to succeed him.

of his time in exile. He returned to Petrograd with Kamenev in March 1917, to take over the Bolshevik Central Committee and edit *Pravda*, the party newspaper.

Often overlooked by others, Stalin was once dismissed by the economist and revolutionary journalist Nikolai Sukhanov as "a gray spot which would sometimes give out a dim and inconsequential light. There is really nothing more to be said about him."[83]

Sukhanov grossly underestimated Stalin. Although the future dictator was not a brilliant thinker or conversationalist, he knew how to quietly and stealthily accomplish his goals. He was a vengeful, cunning, treacherous individual who would do literally anything—lie, threaten, blackmail, even commit mass murder—to acquire and maintain personal power.

During the civil war, Stalin had agreed to be general secretary of the Communist party. It was a nonglamorous position, which almost no one else in the party's inner circle wanted. But Stalin understood that holding this office would enable him to appoint loyal supporters to important positions. Once in place, these men would assist Stalin in one conspiracy after another until all the party boss's opponents had been eliminated.

Lenin's Warnings About Stalin

Shortly before he died, Lenin had been troubled over who would succeed him. Although he never picked a successor, he made it clear that he did not want Stalin. In a letter written as his last testament, Lenin warned the party of Stalin's tactics

A Chilling Description

George F. Kennan, a distinguished expert on the Soviet Union, wrote this vivid description of Stalin in Russia and the West Under Lenin and Stalin, *as quoted in Miller's* The Meaning of Communism.

"[Stalin] was a man dominated . . . by an insatiable vanity and love of power, coupled with the keenest sort of sense of his own inferiority and a . . . jealousy for qualities in others which he did not possess. He had . . . an inordinate touchiness, an endless vindictiveness, an inability ever to forget an insult or a slight, but great patience and power of dissimulation in selecting and preparing the moment to settle the score. . . . At the same time . . . he was a man with most extraordinary talent for political tactics and intrigue, a consummate actor, a dissimulator of genius, a master not only of timing but of . . . the art of 'dosage'— of doing things gradually . . . a master, in particular, of the art of playing people and forces off against each other, for his own benefit. . . .

This was a man of incredible criminality . . . a man in whose entourage no one was ever safe; a man whose hand was set against all that could not be useful to him at the moment."

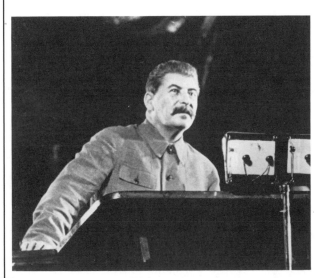

George F. Kennan describes Stalin as "a man of incredible criminality."

and asked that the Georgian be removed as general secretary:

> Comrade Stalin . . . has concentrated an enormous power in his hand, and I am not sure whether he will always know how to use this power with sufficient caution. . . . Stalin is excessively rude, and this defect . . . cannot be tolerated in one holding the position of the General Secretary. Because of this, I propose that the comrades consider the method by which Stalin would be removed from this position and by which another man would be selected for it.[84]

Stalin's Rise to Power

The majority of party members, however, never learned of Lenin's wishes. Stalin had allies, including two top Communist officials, Lev Kamenev and Grigori Zinoviev, who decided to assist the aspiring dictator in destroying Trotsky's bid for leadership. They feared that Trotsky—a hero of the civil war and the leader of the Red Army—might become another military strong man, like Napoleon. But like Sukhanov, Kamenev and Zinoviev had misjudged Stalin. Having underestimated his ambition and power, they thought they would be able to control him. Therefore, Kamenev and Zinoviev rose to Stalin's defense when Lenin's damaging letter was presented at a closed meeting of the Central Committee. They convinced the committee that Lenin's fears were groundless and that his letter should not be read to the general party membership. Not until 1956, when Stalin had been dead for three years, did the people of the U.S.S.R. learn of Lenin's misgivings concerning their tyrannical leader.

The man of steel was now in a strong position to make public attacks against Trotsky's character and motives, thanks to the large number of supporters he had been appointing to key positions within the Soviet bureaucracy. Party meetings were no longer democratic. Instead, as historian Michael Kort points out:

> Attempts to speak against [Stalin, Kamenev, and Zinoviev] at the Thirteenth Party Congress itself were drowned in jeers. It was a new species of party congress, run according to the new Stalinist script. Debate and decision making were banished forever in favor of prefabricated speeches, prepackaged decisions, and organized abuse. Even Krupskaya [Lenin's widow] was driven from the podium

Lenin's successors promenade in Moscow, including, from left to right, Joseph Stalin, Alexi Rykov, Lev Kamenev, and Grigori Zinoviev.

when she tried to criticize the new leadership.[85]

Although Trotsky defiantly fought back with revolutionary-sounding speeches and writings attacking the growing dictatorial rule of Stalin, the web of deceit and lies spun by Stalin eventually proved too entangling. Trotsky's rhetoric made little difference against a majority of hand-picked party officials who always voted as Stalin told them. Eventually, Stalin and his supporters within the party forced Trotsky to resign as commissar [minister] of war. Next they expelled him from the Communist party, accusing him of being disloyal and "too democratic."

In 1928 Trotsky went into exile, ever fearful of what the wily Stalin would try next. Thus, the man who helped destroy the czarist system, win the civil war, and forge modern communism was now on the run, a victim of the very system he had been instrumental in establishing. With Trotsky in hiding, Stalin was free to further the communist revolution his own way.

Revolution from Above

Under Stalin's command, Russia would embark on one of the most astounding transformations in history. It was, as a government publication authorized by Stalin put it, a revolution "from above, on the initiative of the state, and directly supported from below, by the millions of peasants, who were fighting to . . . live in freedom on the collective farms.[86]

Stalin was wrong about strong peasant support; millions of peasants hated what he did to them. But he was right about the

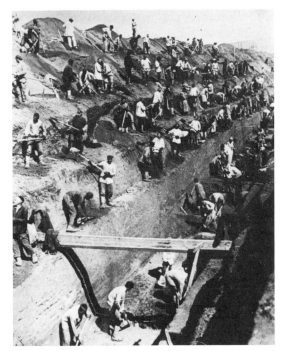

As Soviet leader, Stalin launched massive development and industrialization programs.

revolution coming from above. It was, argues historian Robert C. Tucker in *Stalin in Power*, a second revolution that

> was . . . aimed primarily at making Russia a mighty military-industrial power able to fend for itself in an unfriendly international setting and to expand its borders as opportunity permitted . . . [Stalin's revolution was] not a return to the Russia of the last tsars, but a revival of a state-building process that had occurred much earlier in the country's history.[87]

One of Stalin's first important acts was to rid the country of Lenin's NEP and launch instead his own thousand-page Five-Year Plan. A primary purpose of the plan was to turn Russia into a major industrial country as fast as possible. Stalin hoped industrialization would lead to economic growth and military power, making Russia as powerful as the world's greatest industrial nations.

One of his first steps was to reinvigorate the major government effort to nationalize all major private industries. The production of consumer goods was reduced to make way for an increase in heavy industry, mining, energy production, and transportation. Stalin's goal was a 250 percent increase in overall industrial production, with a 333 percent increase in heavy industry.

To keep the factories humming 24 hours a day, Stalin authorized the use of involuntary human labor. He also demanded that Russians work at a breakneck speed to meet his imposed goals. "The Five-Year Plan in four years!" was a slogan widely used by the government to spur the workers to produce more. No complaints were tolerated. Nothing was allowed to interfere with the frantic attempt to increase industrial production. The Five-Year Plan was a law that had to be obeyed. Stalin's secret police arrested or even executed plant managers who were unsuccessful in the struggle to meet production quotas and goals imposed by the government's State Planning Commission, or Gosplan.

In 1931 Stalin delivered the following exhortation to a workers' conference:

> To retard the tempo—this means to drop behind. We do not want to be beaten! . . . We are fifty to a hundred years behind the advanced countries. We must make up this gap in ten years. . . . Or they will crush us![88]

At first, many party officials supported Stalin's industrial policy. They realized only too well how Russia's backwardness had contributed to defeat and suffering during World War I. If Russia became a mighty industrial power, they reasoned, it would not be punished by its enemies so easily again.

A Backward Nation

Harrison E. Salisbury's classic, Black Night, White Snow: Russia's Revolutions 1905-1917, *contains this excerpt from a speech Stalin made at a conference of Soviet industrial managers in 1931.*

"The history of old Russia consisted of the fact that she was always being beaten because of her backwardness. She was beaten by the Mongol khans. She was beaten by the Turkish beys. She was beaten by the Swedish knights. She was beaten by the Polish-Lithuanian pans. She was beaten by the Anglo-French capitalists. She was beaten by the Japanese barons. She was beaten by all—for her backwardness. For military backwardness. Cultural backwardness. Political backwardness. Industrial backwardness. Agricultural backwardness. They beat her because to beat her was profitable and could be done with impunity.

The first collective farm harvest during Stalin's collectivization campaign.

Industrialization, however, was only part of Stalin's vision. Food was also essential to the new scheme. The growing number of city workers had to be fed. Stalin also planned to bring in foreign capital by exporting crops. To this end, he ordered a vast expansion of the "collectivization" of agriculture begun under Lenin. Russia's 25 million small private farms were to be confiscated and combined into huge government complexes called kolkhozes, worked by fifty to a hundred families who labored as government workers, not private farmers.

The Peasants Fight Back

Many of Russia's poorest peasants did not oppose collectivization. They had nothing to lose by such a change. Other, more prosperous peasants, including the kulaks—who had substantial holdings in land, crops, and livestock—fiercely resisted the government's efforts to take

their property. What had their ancestors fought the nobles over, they demanded, if not for the right to own their own farms? They burned their crops and slaughtered their farm animals rather than see the Communists confiscate them. In 1929 alone, about 18 million horses and 15 million cattle were killed.

When food shortages started to appear in June 1929 as a result of the kulaks' defiance, Stalin switched to a new tactic: the use of terror and brute force to bring about their cooperation. Tens of thousands of political party members and the Red Army were dispatched to the countryside, where peasants were beaten to force them to work on the state farms, exiled, or killed.

The kulaks—who made up 5 percent of the peasant population—were singled out for punishment. Stalin wanted to liquidate them "as a class." This meant murdering or deporting them by the millions. All too often, however, Stalin's men made no distinction between the kulaks and any other peasants, slaughtering rural people

Russia's peasants suffered miserable conditions under Stalin, who relentlessly pursued an unrealistic five-year economic plan.

indiscriminately, or leaving them to die from hunger and disease in the Arctic wastelands of Siberia.

The peasants fought back violently, battling with anything they could grab—clubs, pitchforks, guns. In the end, however, they were no match for Stalin's Red Guards; the government forces crushed all their uprisings, exterminating as many as 5 million peasants in the process.

Within the first two years of the collectivization effort, more than half of all peasants had been driven from their private farms; by 1936, however, 91 percent of all peasants were affected. The Bolsheviks' goal of land reform had become a cruel, mocking memory.

The wholesale butchery and violence led to a devastating famine, which killed at least 5 million more people, and a complete disruption of the national economy. Yet even as peasants and their children starved to death, Stalin's government continued exporting grain to obtain money for the industrialization effort.

Collectivization was a major disaster. Under the czars, Russia had exported food. Now, and for many decades to come, Russia would have to import food to feed its people.

The Great Purge

When Communist party members criticized Stalin in the wake of the disasters his policies had caused, he struck back viciously. He ordered his secret police to begin a purge of "all enemies of the people who sow discord in the [Communist] party."[89] Thus began the terror-filled years of the 1930s, remembered today as the period of the Great Purge.

Stalin had become a fanatical dictator, devoid of human sympathy. Believing that conspirators were plotting against him everywhere, he became suspicious of everyone, including friends and members of his family. No disagreement, no opposition among fellow veteran Bolsheviks was allowed. As a result, thousands of members were expelled from the Communist party. As historian J.N. Westwood points out,

Ruled by Stalin's Will

For 50 years, from Stalin to Gorbachev, foreign minister and ambassador Andrei Gromyko had held high office in the Soviet Union. In this passage from his Memoirs, *he offers a chilling glimpse at how Stalin assumed absolute power.*

"A permanent struggle [for power] . . . was going on . . . [that] became pregnant with danger after the death of Lenin in 1924. . . .

At the very centre of this struggle stood the fateful figure of Stalin. Those who associated themselves with him and his plan slid with him down the slippery slope, whether they realised it or not. With their own hands, sometimes unwillingly, they cleared the path for Stalin and one-man rule, until finally one single individual had acquired the power to decide the affairs of state as he alone thought fit. . . . Those who timidly thought their actions should be guided by notions of justice simply packed their ideas away, generally in order to survive. Stalin was already operating on the principle that the highest law was his own will. Not many tsars had been able to say that."

The increasingly powerful Stalin reviews a military parade in Red Square.

expulsion meant trouble for ousted party members:

> Loss of Party membership often entailed loss of job and unemployability for the former member, and frequently also for his family and friends. Those expelled for ideological reasons faced the possibility of imprisonment or deportation, or both.[90]

Stalin even turned his treachery against the very men who had helped him destroy Trotsky. In 1934, at the Seventeenth Communist Party Congress, several top party officials dared to protest the purges and suggested that Stalin be removed and replaced by Sergei M. Kirov, a popular high-ranking party official. Stalin was infuriated. Not quite six months later, Kirov was mysteriously killed, probably on orders from Stalin. The only witness died in a car crash that many suspected had not been accidental. Stalin then conspired to have Kamenev and Zinoviev blamed for Kirov's death, despite the existence of a confession by another man. The two old Bolsheviks and fourteen other prominent Communist party officials were executed.

More terror and bloodshed were yet to come. Stalin used the Kirov case as an excuse to eliminate political rivals. Thousands of government employees and intellectuals of all types were accused of terrorism and disloyalty. Their penalties: imprisonment, exile, or death. No one was safe from the knock on the door, the phony trial, the firing squad. Not friends, not military officers, not the secret police, not even Communist party members, whose loyalty should have remained unquestioned, were immune from the terror. "Stalin killed more communists than the tsars had ever even arrested," asserts William J. Miller.[91]

Stalin's nightmare of mass murder and torture was extended to millions of others. Middle-level factory managers and engineers were accused of being wreckers and saboteurs of the economy. Priests, teachers of foreign language, factory managers, writers, artists, and many who merely had relatives or friends in foreign countries were condemned as "Trotskyists" and spies. "Almost no one dares have any contact with foreigners and this is not unbased fear but a proper sense of reality," wrote William Bullitt, the U.S. ambassador to the Soviet Union in 1935.[92]

Most of the victims were innocent of any crime. But for the sake of appearances, Stalin's cronies orchestrated mock trials, during which tortured or blackmailed defendants confessed to crimes they had not committed, hoping to avoid the death penalty, or to protect their families and friends. Stalin's victims died by the millions in front of firing squads or from starvation and disease in prison camps called gulags. And in the gulags, Stalin had at his disposal an enormous supply of slave labor. In fact, during the 1930s, an estimated 8 to 15 million citizens—5 to 10 percent of the total population of the Soviet Union—slaved for the Communist state.

In 1931 a group of prominent Britons traveling in Russia had a chance to meet with Stalin. Lady Astor, one of the more outspoken of the visitors, asked the Soviet leader, "How long are you going to go on killing people?"

"As long as it is necessary," Stalin replied.[93]

At one point during the frenzy of state-sponsored terror and death, Stalin's wife Nadezhda Alliluyeva, despairing over her husband's demonic cruelty, committed suicide.

In this relentless nationwide frenzy many citizens publicly denounced friends, neighbors, colleagues, and strangers as enemies of the state, either out of fear or for devious personal reasons. Author Alexander Solzhenitsyn, a former gulag prisoner, recalls:

> They take you aside in a factory corridor . . . and you are arrested. . . . They take you right off the operating table. . . . You are arrested by the meterman . . . a bicyclist who has run into you on the street, by a railway conductor, a taxi driver, a savings bank teller, the manager of a movie theater.[94]

By the late 1930s, Stalin had killed almost every high-ranking Bolshevik involved in the October Revolution of 1917. And in 1940 a Stalinist agent located Trotsky in Mexico and murdered the former Bolshevik hero with a pickax.

When Stalin realized that the purges were destroying the country, he singled out a new group for destruction: the secret police.

The unspeakable atrocities ordered by Stalin began to slacken during the late 1930s, when an external threat from Germany again materialized. Aggression against various European nations and ethnic groups by Germany, led by Adolf Hitler and his ferociously anticommunist National Socialist (Nazi) party, would cause World War II. During the war years of 1939-1945, the Soviet Union suffered enormously, thanks to Stalin having killed or imprisoned 35,000 experienced military officers.

How many people did Stalin kill altogether? Although experts disagree, historian Roy Medvedev puts the total number

of deaths near 20 million, making Stalin the greatest killer in history. "You cannot make a revolution with silk gloves,"[95] Stalin once said in chilling understatement.

Stalin's Imprint on Russian Life

In the process of furthering the Revolution, Stalin was successful in transforming the Soviet Union into a major nation, the only one during his lifetime to rival the United States as a nuclear superpower. Under Stalin, 500 new factories were built during the global economic depression of the 1930s. One-quarter of total coal production came from new pits. There was also a 25 percent increase in the number

The rise of Adolf Hitler and his Nazi party was a clear threat to the Soviet Union, which had lost 35,000 military officers under Stalin's terrorist regime.

While his tactics were monstrous, Stalin indisputably turned the Soviet Union into a great industrial nation. This 1931 photo shows workers assembling machinery at a plant in Leningrad.

of new oil wells. Steel production was increased from 4 million tons annually to 17 million tons. Heavy industry increased by 400 percent.

For millions of Russians life improved on a material level under Stalin's rule. Great gains were made in living standards, literacy, medical care, and nutrition.

But the original goals of the Revolution did not materialize. The basic human rights that millions of Russians had feverishly yearned for were never observed and protected by law.

Stalin, though, did not pervert the goals of the Revolution all by himself. Angelica Balabanoff, a disillusioned Bolshevik, writes that

> without Lenin there would have been no Stalin, even if Stalin was only a monstrous caricature of the founder of Bolshevism. From the very beginning of his career as a revolutionist Stalin embraced Lenin's theory and methods; the repulsive traits he revealed as a dictator were developed under Lenin's regime. The apparatus [government system] devised by Lenin made it possible for individuals like Stalin to develop their innate wickedness.[96]

The Russian Revolution was begun in the name of the people. Russians from all walks of life had dared to hope for land, food, freedom, democracy, and an end to oppression and misery.

Instead, the Bolshevik revolution of 1917 brought to power only another kind of autocrat, more powerful and murderous than any czar.

The Legacy of Revolution

When the Bolsheviks overthrew the Provisional Government in 1917, only Petrograd was communist. Within the next several decades, the impact of the Russian Revolution was far more extensive. What had begun as a massive uprising against the cruel, corrupt, and unresponsive czarist system transformed backward Russia into a major world power, the leader, as well, of modern communism.

In the early days of the Revolution, many Bolshevik leaders believed that a "permanent revolution" was necessary to sustain Russia's attempt to build a modern socialist society. For this to happen, they thought, revolutions would need to take

Portraits of Lenin and his successor in Tiananmen Square in Beijing, China. Clearly, the impact of the Russian Revolution reached far beyond Russia's own borders.

place in other industrialized countries, enabling revolutionaries to aid one another economically and politically across borders. To promote this concept, the Bolsheviks developed the *Communist International* (*Comintern*), an independent agency set up to foster communist revolutions against capitalism beyond Russia's boundaries. From 1919 to 1943, Comintern distributed party propaganda and tried to take control of various worldwide labor unions and workers' groups to promote revolution among workers all over the world. Comintern's efforts furthered the communist movement everywhere. Communists in

The Soviet Union ceased to exist in 1991. The newly raised Russian flag flutters in the wind over the Kremlin, where it has replaced the Soviet flag.

many lands swore loyalty to Comintern rather than to their own countries.

During the twentieth century, communist governments arose in eastern Europe, mainland China, Southeast Asia, North Korea, Yugoslavia, and parts of Latin America, Africa, and elsewhere. At one point, one-third of the world's population lived under governments somehow derived from the ideas of Marx and Lenin.

Communism also found supporters in socialist and working-class organizations that formed in free and democratic countries, such as Britain, France, and the United States. This was especially true during the Great Depression of the 1930s, a period of global economic collapse. At the time, many people thought that the free enterprise system was doomed and believed that the Soviet Union offered an example of a better economic order. Few outsiders then, however, knew the real horrors of Stalin's regime.

In fact, it was the secrecy surrounding Stalin's atrocities and the Soviet Union's economic troubles that contributed to the cold war—a struggle of economic and political ideas between the Soviet Union and western democracies. The cold war fueled a costly and deadly arms race which brought the United States and the USSR to the brink of nuclear war in 1962.

During the cold war, the Soviet Union aggressively tried to export its revolutionary ideas, usually by stealth, cunning, and violence. The United States and its western allies challenged any expansion of communism.

But by the early 1990s, the cold war had ended. A new revolution came to Russia. No longer could Soviet leaders keep the nation's troubles secret. Suddenly, it became clear that if given a chance, the

Since the breakup of the Soviet Union, ethnic rivalries once again trouble the land. Here, a woman mourns the destruction of her house in Moldova, where long-suppressed ethnic hatreds have exploded into violence.

people of the Soviet Union would eagerly rid themselves of the oppression and tyranny created by Lenin and Stalin. They overthrew communism for a chance at what revolutionaries had always wanted—freedom and democracy.

In 1991 the Soviet Union officially ceased to exist. After a brief period of joy and celebration, however, ethnic rivalries, economic chaos, and political unrest once again began to trouble the land. Whether the nations of the former Soviet Union will be able to fulfill the dreams of the early revolutionaries and build a nation that represents all of its people remains an unanswered question.

Notes

Introduction: An Unfulfilled Promise

1. Bruce Lockhart, *Memoirs of a British Agent.* Taken from *The Russian Revolution: The CBS Legacy Collection.* New York: Macmillan, 1967.

2. John Reed, *Ten Days That Shook the World.* New York: Random House, 1960.

Chapter 1: Life Under the Czars

3. J.N. Westwood, *Russia 1917-1964.* New York: Harper & Row, 1966.

4. Quoted in William J. Miller, *The Meaning of Communism.* Morristown, NJ: Silver Burdett, 1976.

5. Quoted in John Stuart Martin, ed., *A Picture History of Russia.* New York: Crown, 1968.

6. Quoted in Ronald Seth, *Milestones in Russian History.* Philadelphia: Chilton, 1968.

7. Quoted in *The Russian Revolution: The CBS Legacy Collection.*

8. Quoted in Rhoda Hoff, *Russia: Adventures in Eyewitness History.* New York: Henry Z. Walck, 1964.

9. Quoted in Richard Pipes, *The Russian Revolution.* New York: Knopf, 1990.

Chapter 2: The Seeds of Revolution

10. Quoted in Leopold H. Haimson, *The Origins of Bolshevism.* Cambridge, MA: Harvard University Press, 1967.

11. Quoted in Emily Morrison Beck, ed., *Bartlett's Familiar Quotations.* Boston: Little, Brown, 1980.

12. Quoted in George Seldes, *The Great Thoughts.* New York: Ballantine, 1985.

13. Quoted in T. Walter Wallbank, Alastair M. Taylor, and George Barr Carson Jr., eds., *Civilization: Past and Present,* Vol. Two. Chicago: Scott, Foresman, 1965.

14. Quoted in Seldes, *The Great Thoughts.*

15. Quoted in Wallbank et al., *Civilization.*

16. Quoted in Miller, *The Meaning of Communism.*

17. Quoted in *The Russian Revolution: The CBS Legacy Collection.*

18. Quoted in Haimson, *The Origins of Bolshevism.*

19. Quoted in Michael C. Morgan, *Lenin.* Athens: Ohio University Press, 1971.

20. Quoted in Miller, *The Meaning of Communism.*

Chapter 3: Taking It to the Streets: The First Revolution

21. Paul and Beatrice Grabbe, eds., *The Private World of the Last Czar: In the Photographs and Notes of General Count Alexander Grabbe.* Boston and Toronto: Little, Brown, 1984.

22. Quoted in Michael Kort, *The Soviet Colossus: A History of the USSR.* New York: Scribner's, 1985

23. Leon Trotsky, *The History of the Russian Revolution.* New York: Monad Press, 1980.

24. Grabbe, *The Private World of the Last Czar.*

25. Trotsky, *The History of the Russian Revolution.*

26. Quoted in E.M. Halliday, *Russia in Revolution.* New York: American Heritage, 1967.

27. Quoted in Harrison E. Salisbury, *Black Night, White Snow: Russia's Revolutions 1905-1917.* Garden City, NY: Doubleday, 1978.

28. Quoted in Salisbury, *Black Night, White Snow.*

29. Quoted in Robert K. Massie, *Nicholas and Alexandra,* New York: Atheneum, 1967.

30. Quoted in *Time Frame A.D. 1900-1925: The World in Arms,* eds. of Time-Life Books. Alexandria, VA: Time-Life Books, 1989.

31. Quoted in Halliday, *Russia in Revolution*.

32. Quoted in Ian Grey, *History of Russia*. New York: American Heritage, 1970.

Chapter 4: The Great War and the Mad Monk

33. Quoted in Alan Moorehead, *The Russian Revolution*. New York: Harper & Brothers, 1958.

34. Grey, *History of Russia*.

35. Quoted in Halliday, *Russia in Revolution*.

36. Quoted in Salisbury, *Black Night, White Snow*.

37. Quoted in *The Russian Revolution: The CBS Legacy Collection*.

38. Quoted in Moorehead, *The Russian Revolution*.

39. Quoted in Moorehead, *The Russian Revolution*.

40. Quoted in Moorehead, *The Russian Revolution*.

41. Quoted in Moorehead, *The Russian Revolution*.

42. Quoted in Hoff, *Russia: Adventures in Eyewitness History*.

43. Quoted in Hoff, *Russia: Adventures in Eyewitness History*.

44. Quoted in Hoff, *Russia: Adventures in Eyewitness History*.

45. Quoted in Salisbury, *Black Night, White Snow*.

46. Quoted in Moorehead, *The Russian Revolution*.

47. Quoted in Grey, *History of Russia*.

48. Quoted in Miller, *The Meaning of Communism*.

49. Quoted in Salisbury, *Black Night, White Snow*.

Chapter 5: An Exile's Return

50. Quoted in Joel Carmichael, *A Short History of the Russian Revolution*. New York: Basic Books, 1964.

51. Quoted in Moorehead, *The Russian Revolution*.

52. Quoted in *The Russian Revolution: The CBS Legacy Collection*.

53. Quoted in *The Russian Revolution: The CBS Legacy Collection*.

54. Quoted in Carmichael, *A Short History of the Russian Revolution*.

55. Quoted in Moorehead, *The Russian Revolution*.

56. Quoted in *The Russian Revolution: The CBS Legacy Collection*.

57. Quoted in Lionel Kochan, *The Russian Revolution*. New York: John Day, 1970.

58. Quoted in Moorehead, *The Russian Revolution*.

59. Quoted in Larry S. Krieger, Kenneth Neill, and Steven L. Jantzen, *World History: Perspectives of the Past*. Lexington, MA: Heath, 1992.

60. Quoted in *Time Frame A.D. 1900-1925*.

Chapter 6: The Second Revolution

61. Michael Kort, *The Soviet Colossus: A History of the U.S.S.R.* New York: Scribner's, 1985.

62. Quoted in Kochan, *The Russian Revolution*.

63. Quoted in Halliday, *Russia in Revolution*.

64. Quoted in *Time Frame A.D. 1900-1925*.

65. Quoted in *Time Frame A.D. 1900-1925*.

66. Quoted in Salisbury, *Black Night, White Snow*.

67. Quoted in Salisbury, *Black Night, White Snow*.

68. Quoted in Carmichael, *A Short History of the Russian Revolution*.

69. Reed, *Ten Days That Shook the World*.

70. Quoted in Reed, *Ten Days That Shook the World*.

71. *Bartlett's Familiar Quotations*.

72. Geoffrey Trease, *This Is Your Century*. New York: Harcourt, Brace & World, 1965.

73. Moorehead, *The Russian Revolution.*
74. Moorehead, *The Russian Revolution.*

Chapter 7: Russia at War with Itself

75. Quoted in Salisbury, *Black Night, White Snow.*
76. Quoted in Salisbury, *Black Night, White Snow.*
77. Quoted in Salisbury, *Black Night, White Snow.*
78. Quoted in Kaye Moulton Teall, *From Tsars to Commissars: The Story of the Russian Revolution.* New York: Julian Messner, 1966.
79. Grey, *History of Russia.*
80. Kort, *The Soviet Colossus.*
81. Isaac Deutscher, *The Prophet Unarmed, Trotsky: 1921-1929,* Vol. II. New York: Vintage, 1965.
82. Quoted in Salisbury, *Black Night, White Snow.*

Chapter 8: Perverting the Goals of the Revolution

83. Quoted in Trotsky, *The History of the Russian Revolution.*

84. Quoted in Miller, *The Meaning of Communism.*
85. Kort, *The Soviet Colossus.*
86. Robert C. Tucker, *Stalin in Power: The Revolution from Above, 1929-1941.* New York: Norton, 1990.
87. Tucker, *Stalin in Power.*
88. Grey, *History of Russia.*
89. Quoted in "The Stalin Purges and 'Show Trials,'" *Bill of Rights in Action,* Vol. 7, No. 4 (Spring 1991). Los Angeles: Constitutional Rights Foundation.
90. Westwood, *Russia 1917-1964.*
91. Miller, *The Meaning of Communism.*
92. Quoted in Tucker, *Stalin in Power.*
93. Quoted in Clifton Fadiman, ed., *The Little Brown Book of Anecdotes.* Boston: Little, Brown, 1985.
94. Alexander Solzhenitsyn, *The Gulag Archipelago.* New York: Harper & Row, 1973.
95. *Bartlett's Familiar Quotations.*
96. Angelica Balabanoff, *Impressions of Lenin.* Ann Arbor: University of Michigan Press, 1965.

For Further Reading

E.M. Halliday, *Russia in Revolution*. New York: American Heritage, 1967. A fast-paced narrative with lively quotations, though somewhat skimpy on analysis and substance. Well-illustrated and compelling, designed to give the lay reader a stimulating introduction to the story of Russia's revolutions.

Lionel Kochan, *The Russian Revolution*. New York: John Day, 1970. Though lacking in anecdotes and dramatic narrative, this book gives a detailed and informative account of the Revolution from the early days of Czar Nicholas II to the rise of Stalin. The chapter on Stalin, however, minimizes the brutality of his regime.

Douglas Liversidge, *Joseph Stalin*. New York: Franklin Watts, 1969. An interesting and highly readable biography that combines primary source material with good story telling.

Henry Moscow, *Russia Under the Czars*. New York: American Heritage, 1962. A highly entertaining, nonacademic panoramic view of Russia's fascinating and often bizarre history under the czars. Well illustrated.

Ronald Seth, *Milestones in Russian History*. Philadelphia: Chilton, 1968. A series of interesting stories, all retold by the author, which focus on various turning points in Russian history.

Kaye Moulton Teall, *From Tsars to Commissars: The Story of the Russian Revolution*. New York: Julian Messner, 1966. Moulton combines great narrative skill with thorough research to provide a riveting and highly appealing narrative that ranges from the Russian Revolution to the cold war era.

Geoffrey Trease, *This Is Your Century*. New York: Harcourt, Brace & World, 1965. Intended for the general reader, this highly entertaining volume explains the big events of the twentieth century, including the Russian Revolution and the rise of Stalin. Good photographs and illustrations.

Works Consulted

Richard V. Allen, Hall Bartlett, and Kenneth Colegrove, *Democracy and Communism (Theory and Action)*. Princeton, NJ: Van Nostrand, 1967. A cold war era textbook focused on philosophical differences between the United States and the Soviet Union.

Angelica Balabanoff, *Impressions of Lenin*. Ann Arbor: University of Michigan Press, 1965. These highly readable memoirs of Lenin provide a deep and well-rounded look at the controversial Bolshevik leader.

Joel Carmichael, *A Short History of the Russian Revolution*. New York: Basic Books, 1964. Very concise and readable, this work delves deeply into many of the complexities and abstractions connected to the Russian Revolution. Draws heavily on the author's translations of the writings of Nicholai Sukhanov, which provide vivid firsthand accounts of the Bolsheviks and the revolutions of Russia.

Isaac Deutscher, *The Prophet Unarmed, Trotsky: 1921-1929*, Vol. II. New York: Vintage, 1965. A vivid and readable academic account of Trotsky by one of the premier historians of Russia.

Clifton Fadiman, ed., *The Little Brown Book of Anecdotes*. Boston: Little, Brown, 1985. A compilation of amusing and insightful anecdotes about famous people in history.

Paul and Beatrice Grabbe, eds. *The Private World of the Last Czar: In the Photographs and Notes of General Count Alexander Grabbe*. Boston and Toronto: Little, Brown, 1984. Providing observations and photographs, this book renders a personal and at times sympathetic view of Nicholas II and his immediate family.

Ian Grey, *History of Russia*. New York: American Heritage, 1970. A sweeping narrative of Russia's history from its origins to the late 1960s, this work is rich with primary sources, old photographs, and maps.

Andrei Gromyko, *Memoirs*. Translated by Harold Shukman, Garden City, NY: Doubleday, 1989. The recollections of a statesman who served the Soviet Communist regime for more than fifty years provide fascinating insights. Caution should be used, however, in relying on the words of one who was part of a government that suppressed the free speech of others.

Leopold H. Haimson, *The Origins of Bolshevism*. Cambridge, MA: Harvard University Press, 1967. A highly scholarly and informative examination of the various thinkers and their theories of Russia's revolutionary intelligentsia.

Rhoda Hoff, *Russia: Adventures in Eyewitness History*. New York: Henry Z. Walck, 1964. A compilation of short articles, essays, and sketches written by those who witnessed important events in Russian history.

Michael Kort, *The Soviet Colossus: A History of the USSR*. New York: Scribner's, 1985. A scholarly, yet highly readable and entertaining history of the Russian Revolution and the Communist empire it spawned.

Larry S. Krieger, Kenneth Neill, and Stephen L. Jantzen, *World History: Perspectives of the Past*. Lexington, MA: Heath, 1992. A high school textbook that provides a current, comprehensive survey of world history for young adults.

John Stuart Martin, ed., *A Picture History of Russia*. New York: Crown, 1968. An abundance of old photographs and pictures accompanied by a bare, but accurate text.

Karl Marx and Friedrich Engels, *The Communist Manifesto*. New York: Modern Reader Paperbacks, 1964. Fiery and thought-provoking. This classic socialist treatise and call to arms for the working class is brief and quite readable, but requires a developed knowledge of world history.

Robert K. Massie, *Nicholas and Alexandra*. New York: Atheneum, 1967. An extremely well-written examination of Russia's last royal couple. This engrossing narrative is filled with lengthy excerpts from diaries, letters, and other primary sources.

William J. Miller, *The Meaning of Communism*. Morristown, NJ: Silver Burdett, 1976. A textbook filled with anecdotes and primary sources tracing the rise of Marxism to the emergence of the Soviet empire.

Alan Moorehead, *The Russian Revolution*. New York: Harper & Brothers, 1958. This very readable and well-organized book tells the story of the Revolution in a dramatic form.

Michael C. Morgan, *Lenin*. Athens: Ohio University Press, 1971. A scholarly work concentrating on the mind and actions of V.I. Lenin.

Albert P. Nenarokov, *Russia in the Twentieth Century: The View of a Soviet Historian*. Translated by David Windheim, New York: Morrow, 1968. A scholarly appraisal of the Revolution from a Soviet historian. Insightful and illuminating in many places, this Communist-era work, however, is conspicuously soft in its treatment of Soviet brutality.

Richard Pipes, *The Russian Revolution*, New York: Knopf, 1990. A detailed and scholarly work by a highly praised U.S. academician. Recently published and up-to-date.

Maria Rasputin and Patte Barham. *Rasputin: The Man Behind the Myth*. Englewood Cliffs, NJ: Prentice-Hall, 1977. An interesting, but highly subjective profile of the controversial Rasputin, told by the monk's daughter.

Readings in World History. Orlando, FL: Harcourt Brace Jovanovich, 1990. A compilation of primary sources.

John Reed, *Ten Days That Shook the World*. New York: Random House, 1960. Written by a young Amerian journalist who was sympathetic to the Bolsheviks, this classic remains one of the most enduring eyewitness accounts of the events of November 1917.

George Seldes, *The Great Thoughts*. New York: Ballantine, 1985. A compilation of short passages of many of the greatest ideas in history.

"The Stalin Purges and 'Show Trials,'" *Bill of Rights in Action*, Vol 7, No. 4, Los Angeles: Constitutional Rights Foundation, (Spring 1991).

Time Frame A.D. 1900-1925 The World in Arms, eds. of Time-Life Books. Alexandria, VA: Time-Life Books, 1989. A major section of this book provides a well-written, though highly compressed, account of the Russian Revolution.

The Russian Revolution: The CBS Legacy Collection. New York: Macmillan, 1967. A compilation of excerpts from classic works on the Russian Revolution.

Alexander Solzhenitsyn, *The Gulag Archipelago*. New York: Harper & Row, 1973.

Leo Tolstoy, *Writings on Civil Disobedience and Nonviolence*. Philadelphia: New Society Publishers, 1987. A collection of essays by one of Russia's greatest writers, including those focusing on Russia's social and economic collapse in the early 1900s.

Leon Trotsky, *The History of the Russian Revolution*. New York: Monad Press, 1980. Although very subjective and partisan, this academic work offers a powerful account by one of the giants of the Revolution.

Considered a classic literary and historical work. No photographs.

Robert C. Tucker, *Stalin in Power: The Revolution from Above, 1928-1941*. New York: Norton, 1990. Scholarly, yet dramatic examination of Stalin and the modern Soviet power structure.

J.N. Westwood, *Russia 1917-1964*. New York: Harper & Row, 1966. An objective and concise book for the general reader.

T. Walter Wallbank, Alastair M. Taylor, and George Barr Carson Jr., eds., *Civilization: Past and Present*, Vol. Two. Chicago: Scott, Foresman, 1965. An unusually readable college-level textbook, with many illuminating excerpts and passages from primary sources on the Russian Revolution.

H.G. Wells, *The Outline of History*. New York: Garden City Publishing, 1931.

Index

Kaplan, Fanny, 81-82
Kennan, George F.
    on Stalin, 89
Kerensky, Alexander
    Bolsheviks and, 67, 72
    denounces Lenin, 60
    directs war efforts, 61-62
    Duma and, 55
    flees revolution, 68
    loses power, 63-64
Kirov, Sergei M., 96
kolkhozes, 93
Kornilov, Lavr G., 63, 64, 65
Krupskaya, Nadezhda K. (Lenin's
    wife), 29, 90-91

Latvia
    forms new country, 77
    freedom from czarist rule, 36
    people in Russia, 12
Lenin, Vladimir Ilyich
    announces Bolshevik takeover, 72-
        73
    assassination attempt, 81-82
    brother's execution and, 27
    calls for new revolution, 64-65
    charged with treason, 62
    childhood of, 27-28
    death of, 87
    directs revolution from Geneva, 37
    exile of, 29
    health deteriorates, 86
    leads revolution, 67-72
    New Economic Policy (NEP), 85
    partnership with Trotsky, 61
    plan for Bolshevik rule, 60
    protests Russian involvement in
        war, 59-60
    returns from exile, 39, 58-59
    revolutionary influences on, 27-29
    revolutionary theories of, 20
    signs Treaty of Brest-Litovsk, 73-74
    warns against Stalin, 88-90
Lithuania
    forms new country, 77
    freedom from czarist rule, 36
    people in Russia, 12
Lockhart, Bruce, 8-9

Marx, Karl
    influence on Lenin, 28, 73
    political theories of, 24-26, 29, 56,
        73, 74
Marxism, 24-26, 29, 56, 73, 74
Mensheviks
    dominate Provisional

Government, 60
    formation of, 29
    Lenin and, 59
    Second All-Russian Congress of
        Soviets, 71
    St. Petersburg Soviet and, 37
middle class, 19, 22, 24
Mikhailov, Mikhail, 20-21
Military Revolutionary Committee
    (MRC)
    formation of, 65, 66
    takes over Provisional
        Government, 67-72
Mongols
    influence on Russia, 10-11

Nechayev, Sergei Genadyevich, 22
Nicholas I
    military revolt against, 13-14
Nicholas II
    abdication of, 54
    as incompetent, 29, 30, 32, 37-38
    assassination of, 80-81
    creates Duma, 36-37, 38-39
    February revolution and, 51, 53
    hatred of, 35-36, 50
    military mutiny against, 51, 53
    October Manifesto, 38
    punishes protesters, 32-33
    unpopularity of, 31
    World War I and, 42, 44-45
nihilism, 22-23, 26
Niklayevich, Nicholas, 38

October Manifesto, 38
Octobrists, 39

Pares, Bernard
    on Russia in World War I, 42
peasants
    collectivization and, 93-94
    hatred of Stalin, 91
    kulaks, 84, 93
        extermination of, 93-94
    life of, 21
    revolts by, 12, 32-33, 34-35
People's Will
    assassination of Alexander II, 15-
        16, 23
    terrorism and, 23
Plehve, Vyacheslav K., 33-34
Plekhanov, Georgi, 29
Poland
    freedom from czarist rule, 36
    people in Russia, 12
    revolt against Russia, 74, 77

political theories
    anarchy, 22
    communism, 25
    Marxism, 24-26, 29, 56, 73, 74
    nihilism, 22-23, 26
    populism, 21-22, 26
    Slavophiles, 20-21
populism, 21-22
proletarians, 24, 25, 26
Protopopov, Alexander, 47-48, 50

Radishchev, Alexander, 21
Rasputin, Grigori Efimovich
    assassination of, 48-50
    character of, 45
    influence on Alexandra, 45-48, 50
    political power of, 46-47
    Russian Orthodox church and, 47
    treats Alexis, 46
Rasputin, Maria, 49
Red Army
    civil war and, 82-83
    control of dissidents, 84, 86
    Trotsky forms, 78-79
Red Guard
    attacks Winter Palace, 68-71
    inadequate military force, 64, 78
Red Terror, 79, 81, 83
Reed, John
    describes Lenin, 72
    on Bolshevik revolution, 9, 74, 75
    storming the Winter Palace, 70
religion
    Marx on, 24
    power in Russia 12, 47
Rodzyanko, 47, 51, 53
Romanov, Mikhail, 54
Romanovs
    reign of, 10, 29, 54
    see also Alexander II, Alexander III,
        Nicholas I, and Nicholas II
Rosenfeld, Lev Borisovich. see
    Kamenev, L.B. (Lev)
Russia
    agriculture in, 12, 14, 32, 40
    anarchy theories in, 22
    antiwar protests, 44, 47, 51-53, 57,
        62
    civil war, 76-83
    class system in, 12-14, 17-19
    Communist rule
        economy suffers, 83
        end of, 100-101
        famine, 83-84
        help from foreign countries, 84
        New Economic Policy (NEP), 85

Picture Credits

About the Author

John M. Dunn is a free-lance writer and high school history teacher. He has taught in Georgia, Florida, North Carolina, and Germany. As a writer and journalist, he has published over 250 articles and stories in more than 20 periodicals, as well as scripts for audiovisual productions and a children's play. He lives with his wife and two daughters in Ocala, Florida.